Growing Up In Monterey

BACK WHEN

Marjorie M. Van Galder

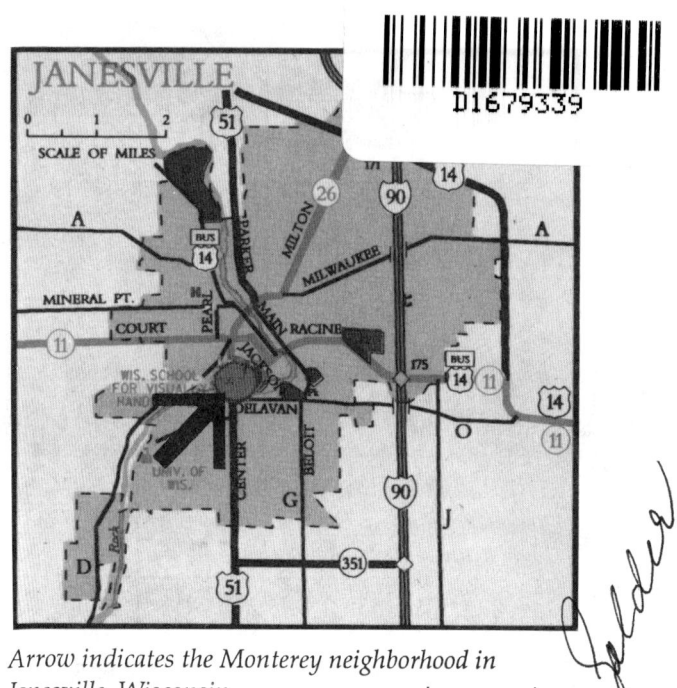

Arrow indicates the Monterey neighborhood in
Janesville, Wisconsin.

Also by the author

Taming The Blue
by Marge Van Galder

TAMING THE BLUE is the eventful story of private aviation as experienced by Russell E. Van Galder, the author's late husband, along with family and friends during the golden years of aviation.

From the thrills of barnstorming to the tragedy of the death of a young female pilot, from stories like goose hunting in an airplane to the contributions of civil aviation to the effort to win WWII, the vast panorama of civilian aviation comes alive.

Growing Up in Monterey

BACK WHEN

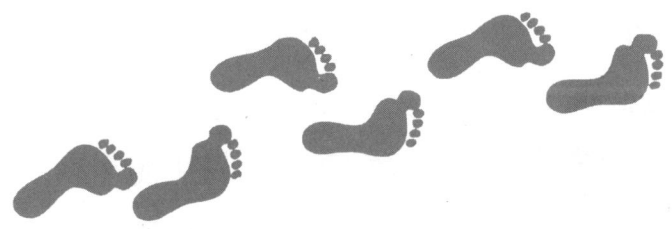

Marjorie M. Van Galder

PLUM TREE PUBLICATIONS

#10 Plum Tree Village
Beloit, WI 53511

Printed in the United States of America

GROWING UP IN MONTEREY, BACK WHEN, Copyright © 1994 by Marjorie M. Van Galder. Printed and bound in the United States of America. All rights reserved. No part of this book may be reproduced in any form or by any electronic or mechanical means without permission in writing from the publisher, except by a reviewer, who may quote brief passages in a review. Published by Plum Tree Publications, #10 Plum Tree Village, Beloit, WI 53511.

ISBN 0-9630187-1-X

Cover Design: Frederick Morris
Map of Monterey: Frederick Morris

Acknowledgements

Many people helped me with the necessary research, Maurice Montgomery, curator/archivist, Rock County Historical Society, was my primary resource. He has a wealth of local history, both in his head, and at his fingertips in well organized files. Thank you, Maurice. Also my appreciation to Cliff Englert, Park & Recreation Dept., City of Janesville; the State Historical Society; Jeff Berg, Wis. Dept. of Health & Social Services; the Beloit Public Library; Sharon Blakely, Janesville Public Library; Fred Burwell, Beloit College archivist; Dorothy Thom Fenne; Laura Roesling Finley; and those kids from Monterey - Les McGill and Howard (Gump) Anderson.

I want to thank the many people who read the book in various stages for their suggestions and encouragement, members of the Writer's Wing, Evelyn Wehrle, Mary Croft, Barbara Vroman, and granddaughter Christina, who also helped me on the computer.

My lasting gratitude goes to John Biester, who agreed to proof read the manuscript but 'couldn't help commenting on the content'. I appreciate his insight and editorial assistance. I was most fortunate to have the helping hand and encouragement of my nephew, Frederick Morris, (Rod's son) who owns a graphic arts studio in San Marino, CA. He designed the book's cover and prepared the map of Monterey, Circa 1920.

During the years I have been writing this book, the person who counseled me, sustained me - even prodded me, was my son, Gene. Thanks, Gene, I couldn't have done it without your help.

Dedicated to my lifelong friend, Ida

*You brought the spark of imagination
and the flame of joy into our lives.*

Contents

	Prologue	1
I.	My Monterey	3
II.	Howling Outside the Gates	13
III.	Imaginative Ida	21
IV.	The Countryside	27
V.	Mulligan Stew - Hobo Style	33
VI.	Worrisome Times	38
VII.	The Five Points	46
VIII.	The Neighborhood Circus	52
IX.	Games We Played	57
X.	City Conveniences	62
XI.	Rainy Days	68
XII.	Looking Out for One Another	71
XIII.	Crazy Daisy	76
XIV.	School Days	81
XV.	The Black Pearl Ring	86
XVI.	Douglas Playground	89
XVII.	The Power of Positive Thinking	95
XVIII.	Spying on the Gypsies	97
XIX.	Summer Vacations	102
XX.	Holidays	113
XXI.	Snow Time	120
XXII.	Clarence	127
XXIII.	A 'Miss Popularity' Contest	131
XXIV.	Our Mean Streak	140
XXV.	The Stork Hoax	145
XXVI.	Diving Off the Bridge	150
XXVII.	Papa's Passing	156

Prologue

During my eight decades on this earth, I have witnessed vast changes in every area of life in America. Not only the knowledge and technical explosion but especially the changing family structure. Questions about my early life by my children, and especially the grandchildren who can't imagine life without computers, TV's, VCR's, and video games - let alone inside plumbing, prompted me to record my childhood memories.

This book relates the simpler life style of a bygone era in the Monterey neighborhood of Janesville, Wisconsin during the years from 1917 to 1926. I reflect on the carefree days of my youth with friend Ida, relate the moral lessons taught at home and at school, note the religious differences in our own neighborhood, and tell how we faced the harsh realities of family illnesses and deaths.

It is my hope that the book will enable readers to better understand the past so as to better understand the present. In today's society we find areas that seem barren, lacking in the simple joys of family, friends, religion and nature. Many yearn for the simplicity and depth of an earlier time.

Follow my footsteps as I relate my experiences; the lure of Rock River, hoboes, tramps and gypsies, games we played, and sharing the totality of life in a different time.

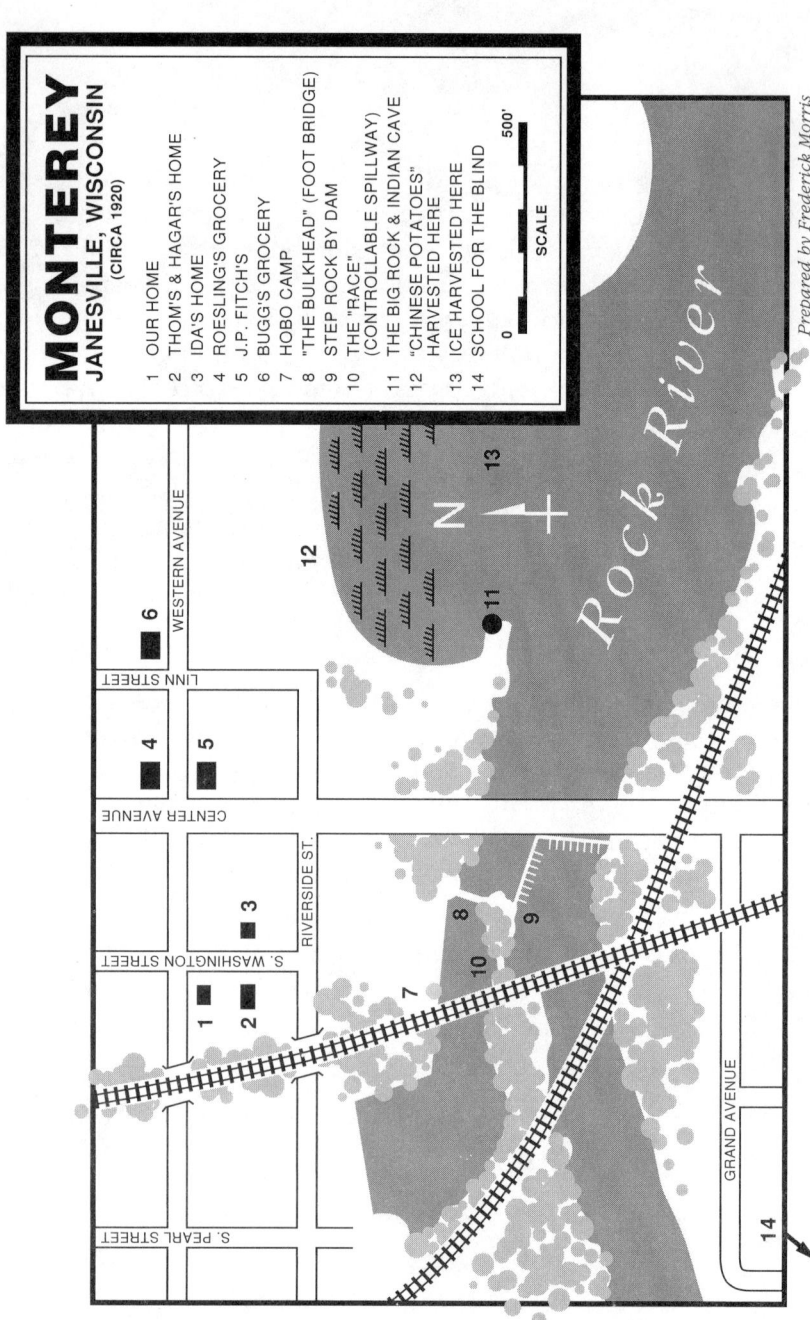

Chapter 1

My Monterey

I grew up in Monterey, a rough neighborhood in south west Janesville, Wisconsin, split by the flowing waters of Rock River, skirted by railroad tracks, dotted with railroad banks, trestles and arches, inhabited by tramps, hoboes, fishermen, and lots of kids. Within Monterey were neighborhoods with their own special name; Snipe Hill, Rock Hill, Spring Brook and others. Away from the tracks, across the river on the east side of town, was The Hill, sometimes referred to as Nob Hill, "where all the snobs live."

In 1849, when Ira Miltimore platted this idyllic area of water, river banks, stately trees and quarries, little did he know he was creating a giant playground for future generations.

In the center was the mighty Rock River, only a block away from our house, with its paths, islands, and pools and the powerful Monterey Dam, that scared us but lured us back. A red iron bridge crossed the river on Center Avenue. Not all of the water flowing under the bridge went over the dam, some channeled its way under an old wooden foot bridge we called the Bulkhead. Here the water picked up speed, raging and churning under the wooden planks on its way to furnish power for a mill below.

Beyond the Bulkhead, alongside the dam, we sat on the big cement steps. Sometimes we fished, but mostly we just sat and watched the water pounding over the dam. My heart beat faster as I watched the powerful movement and force of the

The Bulkhead, a foot bridge.

water splashing rapidly over the dam, fascinated by its colors and noises. Its loud rumbling seemed to warn us to be careful.

On down the path was the Bluegill Pond where my brother and I caught bluegills with a bent pin and no bait. Farther on was the Race, a controllable spillway, where the funneled water raced and churned at a fast pace under the crude foot bridge. As I crossed over the bridge, I tried to stay in the center because it had no railings. I was frightened by the force of the water, whirling and spinning below. Some of the kids threw sticks in. We watched as they rose and fell, spun around by the strong gyrations of the river, a reminder of what could happen if we fell in. Although there was equipment there to change the rate of flow, I never saw it put to use.

Probably because of these hazards, the owners, Wisconsin Power & Light Co., posted a "No Trespassing" sign on the Bulkhead. I didn't know what 'trespassing' meant but related it to the Lord's Prayer. I decided it meant we were not supposed to sin while we were there. It seemed strange to me that this was the only place, even marked with a sign, where we weren't supposed to sin. The sign didn't keep us away.

Others also ignored it and no one ever told us to get out.

Upstream from the dam, past the red iron Monterey Bridge, was Janesville's most prominent and historic landmark—the Big Rock, a limestone promontory that historians said rose 70 feet above the river and was covered with a stand of cedars. (The Big Rock was re-named the Monterey Rock and is now a part of Monterey Park in Janesville's exceptional park system.) Indians used it as a checkpoint to navigate the Rock River. It was a popular gathering place for Indians who fished and camped along the river. As the river was wide and shallow at this point, they portaged their canoes and supplies across to the other side. Early white settlers from the east, who came by foot, walked along paths next to the river. When they saw the Big Rock, they waded across to meet with travellers on the other side.

Hollowed out in the middle of the rock was a cave that Indians and early travellers probably used for shelter. But to us, the Big Rock was another part of our play area. After climbing to the top of the Rock, we peered in all directions

Monterey Dam on a dry day.

The Big Rock, (now Monterey Rock), is Janesville's most prominent and historic landmark. The award-winning painting is by Ernest Rost, well known Janesville artist. It hangs in the Janesville Room at the Janesville Public Library.

pretending we were early explorers. We then decided it was time to scout the cave.

From the top of the Rock, we slid and bumped our way down the steep incline holding on to weeds and vines to keep us from falling in the river. I held my breath as I walked on the narrow, limestone ledge that led to the entrance to the cave. The first one inside, usually our friend Ida, held out her hand to pull the rest of us in over the last big gap.

The cave itself was about 10 feet wide, 12 feet deep and about 7 feet high. The walls and ceiling were etched with initials and crude sayings - definitely not Indian drawings. The remains of a recent campfire in the center of the cave reminded us of recent visitors. Although we always wanted to get in the cave (we figured we were risking our lives to do so), and we planned to play there a while, we never stayed long. We were driven out by an overpowering stench.

"Somebody must think this is a pissin' wall," Ida explained

as we held our noses and quickly made our way out.

Many historians believe the river got its name from the Big Rock, while others believe the Indians referred to it as a river full of little rocks, or "The Rocky River". Anyone who has ever waded the river would probably agree with the Indian version.

Nearby the Rock River with all its natural wonder was our home at 702 So. Washington Street where I lived with Papa, Mama, an older sister, Ruth, an older brother, Rodney, and a baby brother, Donald, who would not live to his first birthday. Along with our white frame house we had an outside privy, a hand pump for water, a good-sized chicken coop and a red, 2-story barn where our Jersey cow, Mollie, resided. Papa rented all this for $25 a month.

At the back of our lot, a high bank led up to the railroad tracks, covered with bushes, trees and rocks, a good habitat for snakes and other interesting creatures. About half way up, a well-worn path stretched along the plateau leading to Riverside Street, then on to the river. Beneath the long railroad trestle that crossed the river, protected by the cement supports and high bank, was a well-populated hobo camp.

The dirt street on the side of our house, Western Avenue, (now Rockport Rd.) had little traffic except for farmers hauling their big cans of milk to the Bowman Dairy in wagons pulled by a team of horses. In the winter, bobsleds were used.

"Mama, Mama, the ice man is coming!" Rod shouted as he ran in the house. The ice man had a regular schedule but Mama sometimes forgot so Rod took it upon himself to remind her.

Mama took a quick look in the ice box, grabbed the red sign and put it in the window, turning it to indicate the number of pounds she needed. The ice man came along, glanced at the sign, then used an ice pick to chisel out the right amount. He picked up the chunk with huge ice tongs, swung it on his padded shoulder, and carried it into the house, placing it in the ice box. On hot summer days the kids swarmed around the wagon begging for ice chips. The ice man usually found

Our home, 702 So. Washington St.

some ice shavings to put in the outstretched hands. The ice was harvested during the winter in nearby Rock River.

One of my chores at home was to empty the flat rectangular pan placed under the ice box to catch the water as the ice melted. Because I waited until it was full, I had trouble easing out the pan without spilling water on the floor.

"Look, Margie, you've got to clean it up," my sister said pointing to a wet spot on the floor—a reminder that I waited too long and it had overflowed.

But the kids didn't pay any attention to another transient to the neighborhood who announced his arrival by calling out in a high melodious voice, "Any rags today, Any rags today!" Sometimes Mama had some odd pieces of material or worn-out sheets that she took out to him. Mama kept a close eye on him as he weighed them on a small scale in the back of his horse-drawn cart. He gave Mama a few pennies before moving down the street singing out, "Any rags today?"

At the edge of our front yard, next to the road, was a big, flat, rectangular rock with a hitching post for tying horses. In the early evening, this platform was a popular gathering spot for neighborhood kids to talk, share confidences, and to listen to our friend Ida tell us stories.

Our white frame house was one and a half stories, with vine-covered porches on the front and side. The kitchen had a big cook stove with a warming oven on top; four openings, managed by lid-openers with fancy coiled handles, and a reservoir on the side which furnished us with a supply of hot water as long as we kept it filled with water carried in from the pump. A worn linoleum covered the floor except for a one foot margin around the edges. A big wooden table and chairs were slightly off center and this is where we ate all our meals. A kitchen cabinet stood by the north wall and the ice box was near the back door.

Papa was superintendent at the Haskins & Schwartz Tobacco Co., on Laurel Avenue, one of many tobacco warehouses in Janesville. The neighbor kids said he was "aristocratic" probably because of his regal bearing and the way he talked. He was 6 feet tall with a muscular but slender body. His straight black hair was cut to frame his well-shaped head and his full, black mustache was always well trimmed. His lean, lined face was serious but his dark blue eyes were friendly. Papa was twenty years older than Mama.

Papa's parents were strict Baptists who didn't condone drinking or dancing, and decreed no card-playing or movies on the Sabbath. Papa was a strict teetotaler by the time of his marriage, although he drank as a youth. He and his three sisters attended Janesville schools, two of the sisters went on to Normal School and became teachers until they married when it was mandatory that teachers retire.

His parents and grandparents all lived in the Janesville area. His maternal grandparents, who first met in this country, were both from Wales. However, because they were born in different regions of the small country, they spoke different dialects and were unable to understand one another. It was a difficulty love overcame with the help of a slate they carried to write notes which they could comprehend.

Mama's father and mother, along with four children, emigrated from Interlaken, Bern, Switzerland, sailing from Le Havre and arriving in the United States on March 1, 1883.

My first cousin, Inez Strauss Spellman, wrote in a family genealogy, "My father, Fred, at the age of seven, had the dubious honor of toting a yellow-enamelled pottie, tied in a red kerchief, down the streets of New York City. Their passage to America was financed by relatives who struck it rich in the California Gold Rush."

Mama was the fifth child, the first to be born in this country, followed by seven more, for a total of twelve - six girls and six boys, including one set of identical twin boys. The children had minimal schooling although they read and wrote well and were interested and informed on national and world affairs.

Four of Mama's six brothers became farmers or cheese-makers, one a carpenter and another owned a saloon. The girls married and became housewives with the exception of Bertha, a beautiful girl, who died at sixteen from tuberculosis, a common cause of death. The families lived in and around Monroe, Wisconsin, surrounded by other Swiss, sharing their customs of wine-making and wine-drinking, singing, yodeling, and dancing. Fun loving, yet hard-working people.

To go from our staid Baptist household to visit Mama's relatives was quite a shock to Ruth, Rod and me. At night we slid out of our beds, crept down the stairs and peeked around the curtain to watch them drink wine, laugh, talk, sing, and yodel. Uncle Chris, Mama's brother, and his wife Aunt Lizzie sang Swiss songs and yodelled. We didn't know what to make of all this merriment. The next day we asked Mama about it and she assured us 'their way' was all right. "People have different customs," she explained.

Back in our block in Monterey, directly across the street from us, lived Katie Bergher. Next to her was the Sievert's, and then our friends, Ida Huber, our ringleader, and her younger brother, Jake. Theirs was a small, one-story, frame house with a barn at the back by the alley. The most interesting feature was a trap door in a bedroom, covered by a large throw rug, that led to the basement. Many times the basement filled with water.

"We have our own swimming hole," Ida said. But that black, sometimes smelly, water didn't look a bit inviting.

On our side of the block there was only one other house, a large stone duplex, where our friends, the Thom's lived. There were seven Thom kids, Walter, Elsie, Millie, Ruth (who was my special friend), Hank, George and Dorothy. They lived in the south half of the big stone house owned since the early 1890's by two sisters Gramma Hager and Gramma Thom.

John and Martha Hager, bachelor brother and spinster sister, lived on the side closest to us. John was a pharmacist in Chicago and returned home week-ends. They were friendly people and often invited us kids to parties in their lovely home. We considered them as worldly and sophisticated and enjoyed sharing their gracious life style.

The land for the Thom home was platted by Hyatt Smith and Ira Miltimore October 23, 1847, later acquired solely by Miltimore. Additional sales were made, and in October of 1849, Horatio Bush sold the land to Clement Dustin for $662.00 at 12% interest, with the condition that Dustin complete the

The Thom's home located at 714 So. Washington St. (recent photo).

dwelling house within one year. At the time there was only a partially completed kitchen on the land. {I like to think this was the Thom's summer kitchen where we played a lot.} After several transactions, the southern part of the land was sold to Ludwig Thom on March 22, 1884, while the northern part was sold to Fritz Hager on February 20, 1893. As I mentioned before, Mrs. Hager and Mrs. Thom were sisters.

It is believed the stone for the Thom home was from Miltimore's Quarry (now the site of Veterans of Foreign Wars Post 1621) located across the river, which played a part in the naming of the area. The workers used gunpowder to blast the limestone. It is said that an especially heavy blast from the quarry created a shattering, staccato racket along with considerable ground shaking. Mr. Miltimore was bombarded with inquiries. With tongue in cheek, Ira Miltimore replied, "You're probably hearing the guns from the Battle of Monterey" (referring to a battle in the Mexican War that had ended several years before). Later, when Miltimore platted the section, he recalled this incident and named it "Monterey".

Monterey—a wonderful, exciting place for kids. All the snobs did not live on Nob Hill, the kids from Monterey were snobbish too, thankful for their own adventuresome world. However, for reasons us kids didn't understand, Mama did not share our enthusiasm.

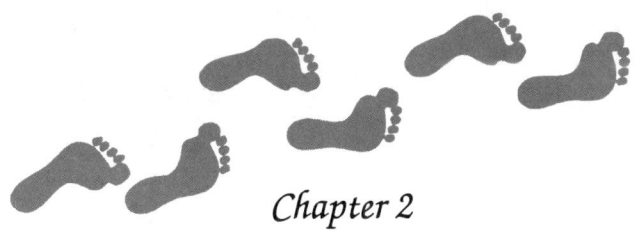

Chapter 2

Howling Outside the Gates

The intrusion of a Catholic neighbor during the illness and death of my baby brother pointed out to me the difference in religious beliefs right in our own neighborhood. I realized these were ingrained beliefs that belied reasoning. Much as I tried to grasp the true story of Christianity, all I found were fragments, confusing and worrisome.

Such as because we were Baptists, my brother, sister and I were not allowed to go to the movies on Sunday. We were told those who did were "sinners". Yet, they didn't look like sinners to us. They were our friends.

On the other hand, Catholics had to eat fish every Friday which, to me, was as bad as not being able to go to the movies on Sunday.

Other things happened that were hard to understand like the time a big Irish girl stole a ring of bologna from Roesling's grocery store. Her bushy red hair gleamed in the sun as she ran down our dusty street defiantly waving the ring of bologna over her head like she was carrying a banner in a parade. A short distance behind, her heavy-set mother chased after her, hair askew, long black skirt flying, her face the color of the bologna.

"Stop Patty, Patty, stop!" she screamed, but Patty charged on. This went on until they reached the railroad arch back of our house. The mother was losing ground.

"Patty, Patty," she shouted, "It's FRIDAY, It's FRIDAY!"

Patty stopped in her tracks, turned back and handed the

bologna to her mother.

That night as Mama was setting the table, I asked, "Is it a worse sin to steal something or to eat meat on Friday?"

"Well, what do you think?" she asked as she turned away to set more plates on the table. I wanted to tell her if I knew I wouldn't have asked her, but I didn't. I didn't talk like that to my parents.

That night after I prayed for my sinner friends who went to the movies, I prayed that Patty would not go to Hell for whatever sin she committed. Then I confided to the Lord, "I'm having trouble understanding the differences Christians have about Your teachings."

Although both the Thom and Huber families were members of St. Paul's Lutheran church, and attended church regularly, they didn't talk about their beliefs. The Thom kids also attended the Lutheran school but Ida and Jake went to public schools.

Some information I heard later from an older friend was also confusing, "The Lutherans go to church regularly and pay their ten percent no matter how poor they are. I guess they're afraid not to, cuz they're scared of God and of the preacher."

We later learned of one Lutheran girl in our neighborhood who was not afraid of her preacher. She fell in love with a handsome young man who was Catholic. He would not leave his church so she agreed to take instruction, turn Catholic, and get married in the Catholic church. (Mama said that the Catholics usually won out in these situations.) The girl's mother wouldn't talk to anyone about it but her eyes were red for weeks while her father God-damned everything and everybody in sight. In planning the wedding, the bride-to-be was upset when she learned she could not have either her best friend or her older sister stand up for her because they were Lutherans.

The parents didn't attend the wedding. "The Priest wouldn't let them," we were told, but later heard that their Lutheran minister forbade them to attend. Although I didn't know what to believe, I did understand the suffering it caused.

Roesling's Grocery, Circa 1917, often shunned by Protestants because the owner was Catholic. Owner, Eugene Roesling, is standing in the doorway wearing a black hat, proudly showing off his delivery fleet of model-T Fords. At one time the Roesling family lived in the flat over the store. The building was purchased from Mr. Roesling in 1946 by the present owners, Case Feed Store.

Why, I wondered, as long as they were all Christians? Why did Protestants walk past Roesling's store, owned by a Catholic, to shop at Bugg's grocery, owned by a Lutheran, and why did Catholics walk past Bugg's to get to Roesling's?

But by far the most worrisome difference was brought about by the illness of my baby brother.

It was the fourteenth day of March, 1917, a cold, blustery day, as I watched Dr. Guy Waufle lean over the crib to examine my brother, Donald Robert Morris, just 15 days short of his first birthday. Mama clung to the railing of the crib, her blue eyes red and swollen, her body limp. The portly doctor straightened up, his black mustache twitched as he shook his head. After clearing his throat several times, he said, "Carrie, we've done everything we can but we're losing the baby. Pneumonia is hard for an infant to fight off."

"I'll stop by the warehouse to tell Bill so he can come home to be with you," the doctor added, "And Carrie, you've got to take care of yourself, you're all worn out." He picked up his worn black leather satchel, positioned his black top hat and left the house. He climbed heavily into the small black buggy and picked up the reins. One flick of the whip and the horse jerked away sending up a spray of dust.

Across the street, Katie Bergher, peering through a hole in the curtain, saw the doctor leave. Katie, a lonesome, elderly widow, spent most of her time in the rocking chair at her front window discreetly shielded by the lace curtains. With rosary beads in hand and a prayer on her lips, she kept the neighborhood under close surveillance.

As soon as Katie saw the doctor's buggy round the corner, she tucked her beads in her pocket, grabbed her heavy black shawl and waddled across the street.

"Carrie, how is the baby?" she asked breathlessly, her puffy eyes squinting at the baby.

Mama shook her head slowly, making no sound.

"Carrie, has the baby been baptized?" Katie asked anxiously.

"No, he hasn't been baptized. You know full well that

Baptists wait until a child is old enough to make his own declaration of faith!" I could tell Mama was annoyed and uneasy.

"Carrie, Carrie," Katie shouted excitedly, "Baby Donnie must be baptized or his little soul will forever howl outside the Gates of Heaven thirsting for water which he will never find."

Mama shook her head. " Katie you know I was brought up a Lutheran and was baptized as an infant but Bill and I are Baptists now and he doesn't believe in baptizing infants."

Katie's eyes rolled and her voice screeched higher and higher, "He must be baptized or any time you put your head on a pillow, you'll hear your baby howling and howling to be saved!"The way she said 'howling' sent shivers through me. I held tighter to Mama's apron.

"Bill would not approve and you know it," Mama said.

"This is no time to worry about Bill. It's the baby who needs to be saved. I'll do it right now!" Katie insisted.

Mama sighed. She sat down clutching the sick baby close to her. I stood next to Mama, as we watched Katie clear a small table leaving the white linen scarf. She lit a small candle, placing it on the table. Then she dipped water from the stove reservoir into a glass bowl and carried it to the table.

Wild-eyed and flushed, Katie mumbled and chanted some verses which I didn't understand as her pudgy hand went back and forth over the bowl of water. She dipped her fingers slowly into the water.

"Bring the baby, Carrie." Mama held the baby while Katie touched the top of his head with her dripping fingers making the sign of the cross.

"I now baptize thee, Donald Robert Morris, in the name of the Father and of the Son and of the Holy Ghost. You are now free of sin and ready to enter the Gates of Heaven."

Suddenly the back door opened and Papa rushed in. "How is our Donnie?" With one look around, he realized what had happened.

"Katie, what did you do to our baby?" he screamed as he

grabbed the table scarf sending the bowl of water and candle crashing to the floor.

"I saved him from Hell, that's what I did." she shouted.

"You old busybody. You hypocrite - you're not making a Catholic out of my son," he shouted. "Get out of here and don't you ever set foot in this house again!" Papa, usually refined and reserved, was beside himself. His face was beet red.

Katie tilted her head defiantly. Slowly she wrapped the shawl around her heavy body, as though covering herself with the robe of God's righteousness. She stalked out the door.

Papa went into a rage when a Catholic neighbor baptized my baby brother Donnie, shown above, who was dying of pneumonia.

"How could you let her do that?" Papa turned to vent his rage on Mama. "How could you?" he asked. "I don't believe it!"

Mama, heartbroken and weak from caring for the sick child, carried the limp form to the bedroom placing him carefully in the crib. She sat down resting her head in her hands.

Papa followed her. "Carrie, stop and think. How could you believe that old witch? What kind of a Lord would punish this innocent child? God is good," he persisted.

"No he isn't, Bill. He's a wrathful God who punishes those who don't obey," she countered, remembering the words of her Lutheran pastor.

"No, no, Carrie. God is merciful and caring."

"I just don't know what to believe any more," Mama wailed. Papa took a deep breath. He leaned over the crib, rubbing his hand lightly over the baby's pale face. He looked at Donnie for a long time, then straightened up. He turned to Mama, touched her lightly on the shoulder and walked to the other room.

"It's time for you kids to get to bed," he said, not looking at us.

I ran upstairs, threw myself on the bed and cried. I cried because Donnie was dying; I cried because Mama was sad; I cried because Papa and Mama were arguing; but, most of all, I cried because I was scared, worried about what would happen to me if I died before I was baptized.

I knelt by the side of the bed,

> *Now I lay me down to sleep,*
> *I pray the Lord my soul to keep;*
> *If I should die before I wake,*
> *I pray thee, Lord, my soul to take.*

Back in bed, I felt myself floating endlessly in the black space outside the lights of the heavenly gates, howling and howling.

The next day Donnie gasped for air for the last time. The laughing baby with the big, sparkling blue eyes was gone.

Window shades were pulled plunging the house into darkness.

"Ssh, ssh, be quiet," we were told.

The undertaker put a black cloth on our front door to let people know a dead person was in the home.

Two days later, graveside services were held in Oak Hill cemetery. The wind howled through the tall trees as they lowered the small box into a hole dug at the foot of my grandmother's grave. If only the wind would stop howling, I thought as I wrapped myself in the folds of Mama's black wool skirt.

That night, after I recited my usual prayer, I made a special plea for Donnie and Mama. I climbed into bed thinking of Donnie and what a good baby he had been and how we were going to miss him. I was sure he had gone straight to Heaven.

But I couldn't help wondering if his passage was smoother because of Katie.

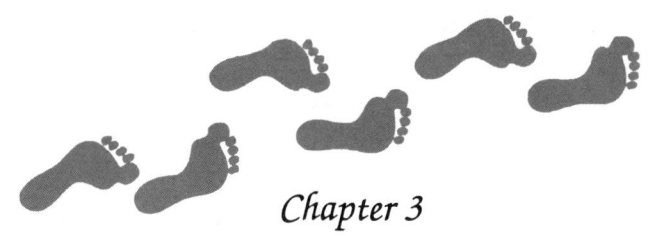

Chapter 3

Imaginative Ida

"Marge, it's your turn to go in. Remember, don't use your own name," Ida whispered.

I was scared. I dug my toe in the dirt road and looked at my sister. She was always bossing me, telling me what to do, but today her face was blank. If she didn't stop me, I knew I had to do it if I wanted to be part of the gang.

Ida nudged me,

"Don't think about it, just do it!"

My feet were heavy as I climbed the high cement steps. I wondered if I was breaking the law, if I might get arrested. I pulled open the heavy door and walked directly to the opening in the caged area lined with bronze.

"Is there a letter for me in General Delivery?" I asked, standing on tiptoe. I felt my face burning.

"I'll see," she said, "What is your name?"

She leaned forward peering down at me through wire-rimmed glasses. The way she stared at me I felt sure she would recognize me wherever, and whenever, she might see me again.

"It-it's Mary Black," I stammered.

She reached for a packet of mail, carefully checking each piece as she went through the pile of envelopes.

"I'm sorry, Mary, there isn't any mail for you today. Maybe something will come tomorrow," she said. Her voice was serious but her eyes smiled.

"Thank you," I said as I ran for the door.

I wondered if she was on to our game—a weekly hike to the Afton Post Office, taking turns to go in, to ask for mail.

As usual, that morning Ida had come calling for us.

"Ruth, Rod, Marge, c'mon out!" she yelled.

The minute we heard Ida holler, the three of us jumped up, ready to run out the kitchen door. But Mama had a different idea.

"You sit right down and finish your breakfast. Ida can wait a few minutes." She stood with hands on hips, an exasperated look on her face. "You kids jump any time Ida calls."

We knew it was true. Ida always thought up fun things to do, sometimes told us stuff we weren't supposed to know and led us on exciting hikes along Rock River and the countryside.

"C'mon, hurry up!" Ida bellowed impatiently.

We slurped down the rest of our oatmeal and milk and rushed out the door, impatient to learn what Ida had in mind for us.

"Guess what we're gonna do today?" Our ringleader, Ida, was always coming up with fun things to do and telling us things we weren't supposed to know.

Ida was born in Switzerland and came to this country with her parents as a small child. As her parents both worked, she was expected to do certain chores around the house and get supper started. Using a Tom Sawyer approach, she enlisted our help. We believed she was bestowing upon us a special privilege, the opportunity to do her work. We didn't even care that while we were dusting and sweeping, star-struck Ida sat in an easy chair in the living room reading the latest movie magazine.

Although we thought it was great, Mama was not pleased. "You go over and clean Ida's house, peel vegetables and wash dishes, but you don't help a bit around here."

We never could make Mama understand what was fun at someone else's house with no grown-ups around was no fun at all at home.

We didn't go in Ida's house when her father was home. He was not fat, but portly, wore thick glasses and rode a skinny bike too small for his heavy body. Like many of the immigrants, he was frugal and determined to accumulate property and a savings account. While he was always grouchy, Ida's mother was personable and friendly.

Ida's younger brother, Jake, was born in this country. He was about my age. He had dark skin and curly dark hair. His head was permanently cocked to one side on his big shoulders. I always liked him but he didn't play with us a lot. He preferred to be with the older boys. On the other hand, my handsome brother, Rod, had to play with his sisters.

"Those big boys are too rough," Mama told him, "I wish we would move to another neighborhood."

On this morning when Ida came calling, she was waiting for us by the pump wearing a whitish-grey middie and black bloomers. Her dark hair, pulled tightly back from her plump, round face, hung in thick braided pigtails. She was dark complexioned, sort of olive-skinned, which I thought was because she drank coffee with evaporated milk in it. She didn't smile much. When she did, her eyes lit up but her mouth was straight in a grin that barely showed a trace of her teeth. Her soft voice had no trace of Swiss accent although her parents spoke only in their native tongue.

"Dutchy looking" is how one neighbor described her, but that wasn't how we saw her. To us, she had an aura about her, a mystique. She was a few years older and knew everything that was going on in the neighborhood. Even though she sometimes played with the older kids, we knew she liked us and enjoyed being with us.

"We're gonna hike to Afton to ask for mail this morning. Jake is coming and so are the Thom's," she told us.

Ida got the idea of asking for mail at Afton when she watched a Hobo walk up to the General Delivery window at the Janesville post office and ask if there was any mail for him. " He went out with a whole bunch of mail," she told us.

Soon the Thom kids and Jake joined us and we started out Western Avenue, under the arch, past Carlsons, under another arch, and over the railroad track on our 8-mile trek to the village of Afton. Besides the post office, which was located in the general store, there was a church, a mill, a lumber yard and some houses. With a destination in mind, we didn't loiter. We walked along kicking up the dust as we followed Ida.

When we reached the store, we all gathered around Ida to see who she would pick to send inside. Ida was always fair in selecting who should go in but I was hoping it wouldn't be me.

But it was, and that prompted my reluctant trip up the high steps to ask for mail.

On the way home, Ida led us off the road into a farmer's field, cautioning us to be quiet.

"I'm gonna show you a Haunted House," she whispered in a scary voice.

After creeping quietly for about five minutes, Ida held up her hand, motioning for us to stop.

"D'ya see that?" she whispered, pointing out the remains of an old stone house. Part of one wall and the chimney were still standing along with the remains of the foundation. We looked into the cellar exposed before us. Two maple trees were in the back and several lilac bushes formed a big clump near the front.

"One night a farmer and his wife were sitting in there by a window, reading the Bible by the kerosene lamp on the table. Someone came along, stood right out here and fired two shots. When the neighbors found them, each one had a bullet in the head that killed them," Ida told us in a hushed voice.

"No one would live in the house so it just crumbled away. Don't get too close. Y'know it's haunted," Ida continued as she looked behind her and around the field.

"Y'know the killer was never found but the police think he's hiding out right around here," Ida wheezed, as she turned her

Ida in a serious mood when she was confirmed at St. Peter's Lutheran Church.

head to look cautiously over her shoulder.

"Ida. you're lying. You're just saying that to scare us," my sister Ruth shouted. But that didn't stop us from racing back to the road.

Walking along at a fast pace, we were getting hotter and hotter. Ida said, "Let's stop at Wiggin's Creek and cool off."

We turned off the road, headed for the deepest part of the creek and jumped in with all our clothes on. After we swam and got cooled off, we splashed water on the clay bank to get it slippery. We crawled up and slid down; up and down; splashing, sliding and skidding, sitting up, laying down, frontwards, backwards and belly flops for hours.

The farmer told Papa about us playing there, which we overheard him repeat to Mama, "They play there for hours. You'd think they were a passel of otters."

As the sun was going down, we knew it was time to head for home. "Let's take some of this clay home for Mama. She likes to put it on her face," Rod suggested. He was always thinking of Mama.

Rod and I dug into the clay with our fingers, working until we each had a small ball. With peace tokens in hand, we joined the motley, bedraggled group and headed for home knowing that tomorrow, with Ida, would be yet another fun day.

Chapter 4

The Countryside

"Rod, Ruth, Marge, c'mon out. We're going hiking."

We heard Ida calling as we sat at the table just finishing our breakfast.

"Your Pied Piper calleth. Where she leadeth, you will follow," Mama sighed, shaking her head. "Tell her to bring you back safe and sound." Before the day was over, her words would haunt me.

Ida was indeed a Pied Piper. She opened our eyes to the wonders around us, "Oh, look at that. Isn't it just beautiful?" She noticed everything and made sure we did too. Her wild imagination spiced up our vision of the countryside.

Standing on a mound in the field, she said, "Look. Look at the cloud shadows racing over the ground. I'll bet they're having a race." We watched the dark patches move across the field, then disappear. As more appeared, the race continued.

Ida pointed to another field, "Look how the tall, yellow grass is swaying. It's dancing. I wonder what's making it do that? Even though we knew it was the wind, it was fun to imagine there was a magical force, a tide or magnetic pull, directing its movement.

Lying down on our backs in the tall grass, we watched the clouds overhead. "What does that cloud remind you of?" Suddenly, all sorts of forms appeared: animal, mythical, human. We compared our discoveries.

"Do you see that one little cloud back there?" Ida asked. "Well, she's in love with that big cloud over there and he isn't paying any attention to her. Do you see how he keeps sailing along, never looking back and she keeps following along? I wouldn't be surprised if she starts to cry and then the raindrops will fall."

In the sunny pastures, she pointed out the Black-eyed Susans, gorgeous, prickly, purple thistles, goldenrod and the fragrant, fragile wild roses that grew in abundance.

"I'm gonna pick some of these roses for Mama," Rod said.

But we learned they drooped in a short time. So, we smelled them, sometimes felt their soft petals, careful not to touch the sharp thorns, admired them, but left them.

In the wooded area, it was ferns, Jack-in-the-Pulpits, ("You know he's preaching a fine sermon", Ida said.), violets, buttercups and the graceful shooting stars. In the swampy places, we found pussy willows, cattails, and some pretty flowers we called orchids.

Ida shared her fascination of trees; the irregularity and color of the bark, the trunk, the outline of the branches, and the shape of the leaves. Then there was the harvest. We loved the shiny acorns and carried some home to play with. We made faces on them, giving them names. But Ida reminded us, "The squirrels bury these and they grow up to be a mighty oak tree." When we picked hickory nuts, Mama spent hours picking out the meats then made fudge or cake for us. We also picked walnuts, sometimes hazelnuts or elderberries from bushes.

But, by far, our favorite trees were in Courtney's apple orchard by the curve on Afton road, just off Western Avenue. The Courtney's never yelled at us or chased us out, possibly because Papa told us to only take the ones that had dropped to the ground. (For many years I thought all "Courtney" apples were from this orchard.)

Walking along the countryside, we felt free to go wherever we wanted to, including farmers' fields and pastures. The only danger was getting in a field with a bull. Each farmer had his own bull for breeding; vicious, ill-natured creatures that would attack their owners as well as kids happening by.

The most interesting bull belonged to Wehinger's off Western Avenue. Interesting because every time we saw it snorting and pawing, Ida had a different tale to tell about it.

"His name is 'Johanna of Beauty Battles'." (We didn't question its name, even though we thought it a strange name for a ferocious bull.} "It's a prize bull, registered and everything, but is he mean!" Whenever we passed the farm, Ida had a new, and yet another hair-raising episode to tell us about Johanna. How the family farm dog, a highly intelligent Collie, saved the young daughter from certain death after the bull had her down. How the owner's wife, seeing her husband being attacked, took off her red skirt and waved it to distract the wicked, bloodthirsty Johanna from finishing off her husband. And, how it gored the hired man, killing him. We might not have believed all of Ida's bull stories but we learned enough to keep our distance from the ferocious beasts.

Hiking with Ida wasn't all nature study or bull stories, she had a knack of providing excitement.

"Come on now, just walk in the middle between the tracks," she told us as we approached the railroad trestle south of Western Avenue over an old quarry.

Following the other kids, I carefully stepped out on the trestle. I looked down through the space in the railroad ties. It was a long way down. The back of my neck tingled. I started to shake.

"Don't think about it, just do it!" Ida called out from her lead position.

This was our first big trestle. All of us were reluctant and scared. My legs felt as though they didn't belong to me as I wavered forward another few steps. Jake, who was walking next to me, pointed out several crows, cawing and circling overhead,

"They're waiting for us to fall so they can pick our bones," he said.

A moment later, Jake tripped and lunged forward. He fell across the track, the lower part of his body dangled over the edge of the narrow trestle as he clung onto the track with both hands.

The girls all gasped and screamed. But not Ida. She glared at her brother sprawled dangerously on the brink.

"Jake Huber, you did that on purpose. Now cut it out and get up here," Ida snapped.

"I did not!" Jake protested.

We knew Jake wasn't afraid of anything. He was always doing dumb, risky things, so we believed Ida, who helped her brother up. We kept on going.

When we were nearing the half-way point, Ida had an important reminder, "We can't tell if a train is coming because of the curve ahead. Hank, you put your ear to the track and tell us if you hear anything," Ida said.

We watched as Hank got down and put his ear to the track. We saw his face turn paper white and he began to tremble.

"I hear a rumble," he managed to say.

We all turned to run back to safety. All except Hank.

"Help, help me. My foot is stuck and I can't get up!" he cried.

His older sister, Millie, ran to him, pulled on his foot but couldn't get it free.

"Wiggle it. Pull as hard as you can!" she shouted.

With shaky fingers, she untied his shoe and took it off. She jerked at his foot and it came free. She helped him up, grabbed the shoe, and they hopped back to where we were standing at the edge of the trestle like they were in a three-legged race, We grabbed them, thankful they made it before the train came.

But no train came. We waited, watched and listened, but the train didn't come.

"That was a false alarm," Ida said, "let's go back over it."

Nobody moved.

"It's all right. Do you see that thing hanging down? Well, that's a safety ladder. We can climb down on it if a train comes and we're caught on the track. C'mon!" Ida urged.

"There's not enough room for all nine of us," Rod said, as we stared at the three rungs on the rusty safety device.

"There's more ladders on the other side," Ida reassured us.

"We've had enough for one day, Ida Huber, and we're not going out there again. We're going home," my sister announced boldly, one hand on her hip and the other wagging in Ida's face.

For once, I agreed with my sister. Besides, I felt sure Ida was just teasing us about going back on the trestle. Anyway,

On our hikes in the country, we usually started out under the arch of this railroad bridge.

on that day, Ida lost her magical Pied Piper powers. Ruth's common sense prevailed. We followed Ruth along the tracks until we reached Western Avenue. We turned onto the road and walked under a big, black cloud. A cool, brisk breeze kicked dust in our faces. Off in the distance we heard a familiar sound.

"Whoo, whoo, whoo," the train whistle wailed in shrill, foreboding howls, "whoo, whoo, whoo."

Mama's parting words popped into my head, reminding me of the story of the Pied Piper and the children who didn't come back. It wasn't only the chill in the air that nipped the back of my neck. I raced for home.

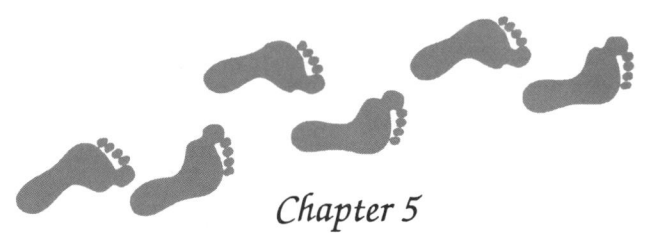

Chapter 5

Mulligan Stew - Hobo Style

Let's go spy on the hoboes; they're probably getting their supper ready now", Ida suggested, after we finished our ball game. Her grey eyes looked from one to the other. She knew she didn't have to say any more. We were ready.

The hobo camp was only a block away on a wide, flat space along Rock River, protected from the weather by a railroad trestle and the high railroad embankment.

With Ida in the lead, we climbed the railroad bank to the plateau, then walked in single file along the path, dwarfed by the tall weeds and brush, until we came to the spot where we had flattened the grass and cleared out the bushes. This was our lookout point, high on the railroad bank, shielded from the hoboes by boulders, trees and brush.

As we looked down from above, we saw about twelve or thirteen hoboes. Some were drinking something out of a can. Ida said it was canned heat and that's how they got high. We watched some washing their clothes in the river, thrashing them up and down. Some pants and shirts were spread on top of the bushes to dry. We knew they belonged to the hoboes who were in their underwear.

"See, they have the fire going and water in the pot," Ida whispered.

Peering out, we watched as they threw twigs and branches on the fire, fanning it with a piece of cardboard. One hobo reached into a gunny sack and pulled out some potatoes and carrots which he wiped with a newspaper before dropping them in the pot.

"I wonder where they got all those vegetables?" someone asked.

"They swiped them, that's where they got 'em," Ida shot back. (If Papa had been there, he would have corrected her, "Hoboes are honest and don't steal. They might beg for food but they're always willing to work for it.")

The smell of the stew and the disappearance of the sun reminded us it was time to go home.

"Before we go, let's roll this big rock down on them," someone suggested. We worked to get the rock loose and in position.

"I'll count to three, then push as hard as you can," Ida commanded. We did as told.

I watched the rock roll down the hill gaining speed as it headed straight for their fire. When it reached the level area, it slowed down and stopped short of the fire, right next to one of the hoboes. The hobo looked up. He looked me right in the eye with an ugly, mean look on his face.

I turned around and discovered, to my surprise, that I was all alone. Apparently, the others ran off as soon as they pushed the rock. I saw the hobo, still in his underwear, coming up the hill. Down the path I ran, scared out of my wits, with the hobo coming right behind me. I ran across Riverside Street and ducked into Thom's summer kitchen where I hid.

A short time later, a neighbor woman came in calling my name. She told me she had watched the undressed hobo chase me.

"He stopped at the edge of the road and watched for a while and then turned back," she explained. She was quite upset and met Papa on his way home from work to tell him about it.

As soon as he walked in the door, Papa demanded an explanation and we had to admit what we had done.

He was furious. Not at the hoboes, but at me.

"Margie, those hoboes never bother you kids. They know their place and mind their own business. I don't ever want to hear about anything like this happening again!" Papa scolded. "They don't have a home to live. They have to keep moving around, riding the rails, trying to just stay alive."

"I'll bet it was Ida's idea," Mama said, but Papa didn't pay any attention to her. Mama always stuck up for us. In her mind, whatever happened couldn't possibly be our fault.

Even if it was Ida's idea, I wouldn't have minded the scolding so much if Papa had asked why the other kids left me up there alone. Especially my brother and sister. But he didn't. I decided he was more worried about the hoboes than me. That night when we went upstairs, I grumbled to Rod, "I wonder if Papa wishes he was a hobo."

The next day Ida called us all together.

"Tomorrow we're gonna have our own Mulligan stew. A real one hobo style. That means we have to swipe all the stuff we use. If you can't steal it, beg for it," Ida told us, "and if you bring anything from any of our own gardens, you can't go with us!" She rattled off a list of what each of us should bring. I was to get the meat.

The next morning I approached the butcher at Roesling's grocery store, "Mr. Dawley, I need some soup bones for my dog."

We lived just a block from the store and Mr. Dawley knew all about our family including the fact that we didn't have a dog.

"Margie, what kind of a dog do you have?"

"He's a big brown dog and he sure eats a lot," I lied.

"What do you call him?" he asked smiling as he held the big cleaver in his hand.

"We call him Spot."

"Oh, that's a good name for a brown dog." His flushed, round face was serious as he chopped away at a big chunk of meat but he looked as though he was trying to keep from laughing. "I think Spot will really like these," he said, handing me a big package.

To get her vegetables, my sister Ruth snuck under the arch and along the railroad bank to get to the back part of Carlson's garden. She quickly pulled up three clusters of carrots then raced pell mell for our chicken coop where Ida had hid the gunny sack. After dropping the carrots in the sack, Ruth rushed in the house, her blonde hair flying, her face beet red. Mama met her at the door.

"What in the world is the matter with you, Ruth? Is the Boogie Man chasing you?" Ruth knew better than to try to explain.

My brother, Rod, had the biggest struggle with his conscience. He went to a garden that was several blocks away, cautiously crept around it several times, then walked down the street a ways. He returned to the garden but could not make himself steal anything. He walked away again, then returned, went up the steps and knocked at the front door of the house.

"My mother wants to know if she can borrow three onions," he said to the startled woman.

"Who are you? Where do you live?"

Rod, who was very shy, pointed in the direction of our house. The lady got the onions telling him he didn't have to return any.

By mid-afternoon, the gunny sack was full.

"Let's go," Ida shouted, tossing the sack over her shoulder. The band of excited thieves, liars, and beggars followed her up the hill lugging a pail of water, a big kettle, and the meat. When we reached the wide area in the plateau, Ida dropped the gunny sack and ordered us to get wood for the fire.

We all scattered to gather wood. Although we hurried, it took longer than we thought. After the fire got going, Ida put on the kettle of water. We thought it would never boil as we sat around watching it. The sun dropped behind the top of the railroad bank, casting an eerie glow on our camp.

"Anyway, it's more fun to have a Mulligan stew at night, just like the hoboes," Ida assured us. We tried to believe her.

By the light of the fire, we wiped off the vegetables with the gunny sack then cut them up. My brother cut his finger and wanted to run home to get it bandaged.

"You can't go home, Rod, you're a hobo and you don't have a home to go to," Ida explained. He stayed.

The stew was just starting to boil when someone bumped one of the rocks the kettle was resting on spilling it and its contents on the sandy soil. Ida picked up the meat and vegetables, brushed them off with her sleeve and threw them back in the pot. Then she added more water. Again we had to wait for the water to boil, then wait for the stew to cook. It took a long time.

"Let's pass the time by singing," Ruth suggested.

"We can't sing. Hoboes don't sing," Ida said.

We finally ended up pretending we were drinking out of a can like we had seen the hoboes do. Finally, after a long wait, Ida decided the stew was ready.

"Come and get it!" she shouted. We quickly gathered around the fire holding out our tin cups. Ida took a large tin dipper, plunged it into the stew and slopped it in our cups. We had no spoons, so we dug the food out with our fingers and slurped the liquid.

"Oh, this is good," my sister said as she wiped the sand from her lips.

"Yeah, this is fun," Hank Thom said as he nervously scanned the dark shadows, "Do you think any hoboes are up on the track spying on us?"

"We'll have to do this again," suggested another as we huddled closer and closer to the fire.

It was Ida herself who brought an end to the Mulligan stew party. She looked around at the faces of the would-be hoboes and said, "Let's stay up here all night!"

It was right then that I was sure I heard Mama calling.

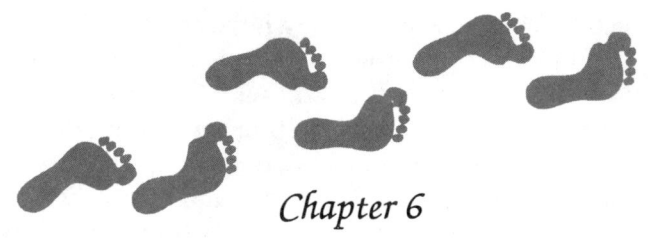

Chapter 6

Worrisome Times

It started out as a beautiful autumn day in 1918.

I skipped alongside Mama on our way to the Milwaukee Road depot at the Five Points to meet Aunt Abby who was coming from rural Juda to help out at our house because Mama had not been well since the death of my baby brother, Donald.

Mama wrote to Abby telling her not to come at this time because of the flu epidemic, but Abby insisted on coming anyway. "I had the flu last fall and recovered in no time," she had written.

When we reached the depot, I walked around the large waiting room with its pointed windows and ornate woodwork, smiling and talking to people. I was feeling special in my Sunday dress and patent leather slippers. My blonde hair was pulled straight back, tied with a big blue ribbon that matched my dress.

"You're such a pretty girl. How old are you?" a woman asked as she offered me a piece of candy.

"I'm five," I said as I thanked her. Just as I started to put the candy in my mouth, everything turned black. I crumpled to the floor and started to vomit. I threw up all over everything, including my pretty dress.

Mama carried me to the wash room and cleaned off my hot face with her hankie. I shivered. My legs wobbled, I couldn't stand alone. When Mama finished cleaning me up, she led me back to the waiting room and held me on her lap. Her happy, blue eyes were now sad as she looked down at me.

"I'm afraid Margie has the flu," Mama whispered to the woman who had offered me the candy.

Soon after, the crossing bells started to ring and the train whistles blew announcing the arrival of the train. The noise made my head hurt even more. People stood up and headed outdoors. Mama put me down on the wooden bench and covered me with her suit jacket. The "candy lady" offered to watch me while Mama went out to meet the train.

"I'm going to tell Abby that you're sick and she must not stay." I could tell she was worried.

Abby refused to listen. "You'll need me now more than ever to help care for Margie. I'm staying."

"But Abby, you have two little ones at home to think about," Mama persisted.

"They're well taken care of and I'm needed here. Let's get Margie home." Abby's jaw was set. The discussion ended.

They carried me home and put me to bed. Mama pulled the shades, plunging the room into darkness. I continued to shiver in spite of the heavy blankets piled on top of me. I hurt all over. Hushed voices floated around me.

Mother sat next to my bed with her head in her hands as the doctor gravely explained.

"We don't know what to do. We don't know how to prevent people from getting it. We don't know what to do to cure it." His voice was soft and tired. He picked up his satchel and wearily shuffled toward the door. "Keep Margie in bed and keep her warm. And, start praying."

After the doctor left, Papa said, "Come sit down a minute and rest." Mama sat down at the kitchen table as Papa handed her the evening paper.

"Oh, Bill, it's just awful. Margie is sick, everyone is sick and soldiers everywhere are dying from the flu," Mama sighed.

"These are worrisome times, Carrie. I see another of our boys died at Camp Grant (Rockford, Illinois) yesterday.

"I wonder if Ernie is all right."

Mama worried constantly about her youngest brother who

was fighting in Europe. Whenever the brown troop trains rolled past our house, Mama ran out, tears streaking down her cheeks, waving her white apron at the soldiers who leaned out the train window to wave back.

"Those poor men going so far away. They're going to be so homesick they won't be able to stand it."

Papa often teased Mama telling her she worried more about the men being lonesome than the real dangers they faced—enemy bullets, getting gassed and now this new strain of flu.

Mama turned the page of the paper and showed Papa an ad in the *Janesville Gazette*.

GUARD AGAINST INFLUENZA

"This dread disease is rampant and every home should take proper precautions to guard against it. One of the best things to do is have a box of Smith's Cold Tablets in the house and at the first sign of sneezing, cold in the head, nose or eyes, take a couple of these tablets.

"Made from an old fashioned formula, they are proof positive against grippe, colds and influenza. Directions on each box.

Price 25 cents — Smith's Pharmacy

Papa grabbed for his hat. "Anything is worth a try," he said as he headed downtown. When he returned, I swallowed the tablets. Later, Mama saw another ad. This one was for Vick's Vapor Rub - advertised as "a sure cure for influenza." Another trip to town for Papa and another remedy tried on me as Mama rubbed Vicks on my chest and upper back.

Enveloped in the strong fumes, and feeling a little better, I was on the cot Mama put in the living room, listening to the conversation around me. My sister Ruth said, "Mary's mother ties a sack of camphor around her neck and she has to wear it all the time."

"That's better than the garlic bags some of the kids wear," Rod said. "My teacher told us that people in Milwaukee have to wear anti-flu masks when they go out. And, they get arrested if they spit on the sidewalk."

"Our soldiers are especially susceptible and are dying by the thousands," Mama said in a low voice. "Some blame the Germans for germ warfare but their men are dying too."

"It's terrible. Coffins are stacked at the depot to be shipped out, and I see a funeral procession almost every day. They're grim reminders of what's happening right here," Papa said. He shook his head. "We're lucky Margie is getting better."

A few days later, on October 9th, city officials throughout the state took measures to prevent the spread of influenza. This notice appreared in the *Gazette*.

> *Theatres, dance halls, public schools, churches, and all places of public assemblage must be closed until further notice. Furthermore, every person is requested and urged to help and assist in every way to arrest the spreading of the disease in our city. Notice is hereby called to the state law against spitting upon sidewalks and in public places, also all persons should observe the rules about using a handkerchief when coughing or sneezing. All doctors are requested and required to report the names and number of patients, and the location of each, to the health officer each day. - Signed, S. B. Buckmaster, Health Officer*

"About the only time people assemble these days is for the War Bond parades and rallies," Papa said, showing Mama an article about the parade in Philadelphia that attracted 200,000 people.

"They have to have rallies to raise more money for the war because us kids aren't in school and can't buy any stamps," Ruth said. She missed chanting "Lick a stamp and lick the Kaiser" when she bought a stamp for a quarter and placed it in her Liberty Bond book.

"It all helps," Papa said, smiling at the importance Ruth placed on the school program.

When my brother and sister were home from school, they read to me and helped wait on me. In about a week, I was able to get out of bed and join the family at the table. Mama smiled as I ate my soup and toast.

But, she didn't smile for long. As I was getting better, Aunt Abby became ill.

"She keeps throwing up and shivering. I can't get her warm. The doctor is on his way," Mama told Papa when he came home from work.

Once again, the doctor shook his head, "The fact that she had the flu last fall makes it even worse for her. All you can do is keep her as comfortable as possible," he said.

A few days later the doctor returned, leaned over Aunt Abby's still body, sighed deeply, then pulled the sheet up over her head. Dear Aunt Abby - who was so determined to help others - was gone.

"It was meant to be," the relatives said as we watched the undertaker take her away in his horse-drawn wagon. Their words didn't console me. I felt it was all my fault because Aunt Abby caught the flu from me. I cried as I thought of 5-year old Stanley and 2-year old Laurabelle losing their mother.

After Abby's death, Mama and Papa took all the sheets, pillow cases, pillows and mattresses off the beds that Abby and I had used and carried them to the back yard. They poured gasoline on the big pile of bedding and torched it. With a loud swish, the flames shot upward.

"Let's hope this is the end of it," Papa sighed.

"It won't be the end for those poor kids without a mother," Mama responded with tears in her eyes as the flames shot higher, smoke curling about her.

When the fire subsided, they opened all the doors and windows to air out the house. They washed everything using a smelly disinfectant. The rugs were carried out and hung over the clotheslines. Papa watched as Mama furiously swung the carpet beater. Whack! Whack! Whack!

Aunt Abby (shown here with Uncle John Strauss in their 1911 wedding photograph) died at our home after catching the flu from me.

"I think she's trying to kill off the demons," he muttered to me. But he didn't smile.

When everything was back in place, the air smelled fresh and clean but slightly antiseptic. The rooms were light as the sunshine poured in.

"Let's hope it's really over," Mama said.

It still wasn't over for me. I even upset Aunt Mayme who turned to Papa in disgust, "What's the matter with that child? Bill, you better talk to her. She can't go on moping forever."

Papa led me into the living room we seldom used and held me on his lap. "Margie, we're not going to have any more of this moping around. It wasn't anybody's fault that you caught the flu and it's no one's fault that Abby got sick. What's happened is over. We can't do anything about it. Do you understand what I'm saying?"

I believed him. Maybe it wasn't my fault.

The next day Ruth pointed out an ad for the Apollo Theatre that also made me feel even better. "Mama, the quarantine is lifted and the theatres are open. Can we go to see Theda Bara in Cleopatra?"

Mama read the ad out loud,

> *To the citizens of this community:*
>
> *During the three weeks the theatre has been closed, we have had ample time to renovate, clean and fumigate. Absolute sanitation prevails. James Zanias, Manager. Oct. 30, 1918.*

"Sounds like our house," my brother Rod said, "Can we go, please, please, please?"

Not ready to take any chances, Mama insisted, "We're going to wait a while longer just to make sure."

About two weeks later, news from overseas pushed aside the worry of the flu epidemic. Papa came home waving the paper with the banner headline. The Armistice was signed.

Thousands of people gathered on November 12 to celebrate the victory. Even Mama went with us to the Five Points where everyone cheered, yelled, clapped and waved flags.

A few days later, Mama received a telegram from Uncle Ernie. "SAFE. RETURNING SOON. TERRIBLY HOMESICK". Mama was right.

That night at supper, Mama's eyes were bright as she announced, "Papa and I have decided it's all right for you kids to go to the show on Saturday."

"Hurray!" we shouted.

Ruth beamed, "The war is over and now the flu war must be over too."

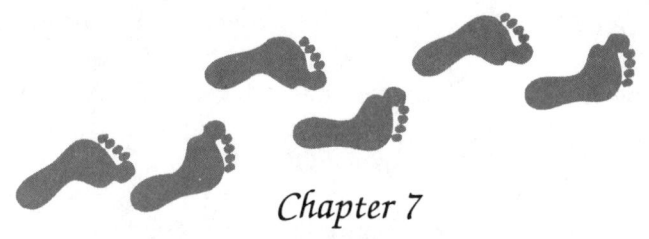

Chapter 7

The Five Points

One of the bigger boys in Monterey was Howard "Gump" Anderson whose father was a mail clerk and baggage handler for the Chicago & Northwestern Railroad. Everything about the locomotives grabbed Gump's attention. Train whistles wailing and crossing bells ringing pulled him to the Five Points, the hub of railroad activity, with the nearby Chicago Northwestern RR and the Milwaukee Road Depots. He liked to tell us what went on there.

When the trains came in, Gump's father unloaded the baggage onto a big iron wagon with four oversized metal wheels, then he pulled it by hand along the brick-surfaced platform back to where the passengers were waiting. Mr. Anderson carried some of the luggage to waiting carriages, provided for use of their guests by the Myers Hotel and the Grand Hotel. Other luggage he took across the tracks to the Milwaukee Road depot for railroad passengers with transfer connections.

"Everybody goes by train, whether to Milton Jct., Brodhead or to New York City. And it's not only people who use the trains, everything is sent on trains. Fresh bread from the bakery is put on and then distributed along the way as well as all kinds of freight, livestock, and the mail," Gump said. He told us that postal workers took the mail to the depot and loaded it in the mail car manned by post office employees who rode the train dropping the mail off at different stations or at railway junctions to be transferred to another train.

We walked up Pearl Street with Gump to see the Roundhouse where workers repaired the train engines. We saw the engine go in front first get turned around and then come out front first. "They maintain the engines here but the men repair and service the railroad cars at 'The Yards'," Gump said. He went on to tell us that the Chicago Northwestern Yard is in South Janesville and that the workers are taken back and forth by small railroad cars. He sounded envious of the men riding in the undersized cars.

Janesville was a railroad division point. Not only were the train engines and cars repaired here but train crews changed at this point which meant many railroad workers lived here. The railroad also hired many Italians for repair of the tracks. They were housed in box cars near the tracks, sometimes as many as thirty workers lived in one car, along with thousands of fleas. One night one of the cars caught fire. All of the men escaped the burning flames, but the fleas weren't that lucky. Neighbors and workers stood around laughing and clapping as they heard the zap, zap, zap as one flea after another met its doom.

Gump watched the dispatcher, listening to the clack, clack, clack of the Morse Code, as he sent out messages. Gump told us how the engineer received messages attached to a high pole, messages that would advise him whether or not to stop at some small village. Small packets of mail were delivered to a moving train with a loop attachment that resembled a tennis racquet.

Gump watched the busy crossing guards, high up in their tower, pumping lever handles to raise and lower the crossing gates. He watched coal tumbling down the chute from the high storage bin above into the engine tender and saw men carrying ice from a nearby railroad ice warehouse to put in cars carrying perishable food.

The Chicago & Northwestern Stock Yard, where cattle were held while waiting to be shipped out, was located near Gump's home. Sometimes Gump went along when his father watered the animals and milked the cows.

During WWI when "Gump" and his friends saw a troop

train stop at the Five Points, they'd yell, "Hey, soldiers, throw us some pennies!" When they did, the kids wrestled one another for them, fighting like demons to get a penny. This amused the soldiers so much that they kept throwing out more pennies to watch the kids rolling around in the gravel next to the tracks scrapping for them. After the train pulled out, the kids all sat down, counted out the pennies, and divided them equally.

Gump liked to watch people get on and off the trains especially vaudeville entertainers scheduled to perform at local theatres. The actors often gave his father free passes for handling their luggage.

"My brother, Ray, and I sat in the front row so we wouldn't miss anything," Gump said.

One evening after attending a vaudeville show at the Apollo Theatre, Gump and his brother, Ray, told their father about the strong man who lifted incredible weights.

"He's the strongest man I ever saw," Gump said as Ray nodded in approval. The boys went on and on about his muscles, his build, and his strength.

Their father listened for quite a while. He looked at them shaking his head, "Yeah, well did you two ever stop to think who carried all his equipment from the train to the carriage?"

Although Gump saw a lot more of the Five Points than I did, I enjoyed waiting at the crossing for the trains to go by gawking at the beautiful people eating in the plush dining cars or sitting in the lavish lounge cars.

"I'll bet that's a movie star," Ida said, pointing to an especially attractive woman. "She looks just like Marian Davis."

Even though we were sure it wasn't, such speculation added to the fun. A few people smiled and waved at us; others ignored us; some pulled down the shades. The big snub!

The railroad workers were different. The engineers waved their big, blue and white gauntletted hands out of the cab, while other workers shouted and waved in response to our greetings. For us, this was a big deal.

My most exciting times at the Five Points were when the

Circus Train came in. Papa woke us up at 4 o'clock. We walked up Center Avenue in the dark so we'd get there in time to watch the unloading. As we approached, we heard the workers shouting orders to one another, then we caught the smells. We watched them move the cage with the yellowish, striped tigers pacing and snarling. Then the majestic lions. They roared, showing off their big sharp teeth, sending a shiver through me. "The one with the full flowing mane is the male," Papa said. We saw the ornate circus cars unloaded and watched in awe as the huge elephants moved methodically in rhythm.

When the train was unloaded, we walked to the circus grounds to watch the circus people get the grounds ready and put up the big tents. It was like a miracle. Each person had a job to do, and everybody helped, including performers. We watched them drag the heavy rope, haul canvas and drive tent stakes into the ground with big sledge hammers. The elephants helped too, as everything fell in place for the big performance.

Later, we watched the big Circus Parade down Milwaukee Street. Horses pulled the colorful, decorated wagons housing wild, exotic animals. Beautiful women in colorful, lavish costumes rode on horses and elephants as well as on top of the circus wagons. A dark-skinned woman, scantily clad in frilly scarves, walked by us with a huge, striped snake coiled around her arm. The Circus Band, in red and gold uniforms, played non-stop as they rode past on top of a wagon pulled by eight white horses. The beautifully decorated caliope wagon signalled the end of the parade. But it's haunting strains hung on, tingling my blood.

After so much excitement, we had to sleep all afternoon so we'd be awake for the evening show. Ida went with us and didn't miss a trick, "If you're gonna buy a box of candy, do it right away because the first ones have better prizes," she told us.

She pointed out the costumes, the acts, and what to watch in the three-ring show. While we enjoyed the circus, Ida was storing up information for putting on a circus of our own.

The Five Points was always an attraction, with or without the Circus Train; fascinating, yet it could be dangerous. Some of the older kids found the Five Points a good place to hop freight cars. They jumped on there, rode down to Western Avenue and leaped off. They knew it was dangerous. Their parents warned them constantly, yet it was a common practice. Us younger kids wanted no part of it, nevertheless, later on, one of our friends tried it and was killed.

His name was Frederick Jonas. He and his family moved into our neighborhood, from Hochuris, Hungary, when he was seven years old. Although he couldn't speak a word of English, "Fritz" as we called him, was sent to Douglas School where we all made fun of the way he talked, his fat, round face and his strange clothes. Although many in the neighborhood were first generation immigrants, it didn't stop them from ridiculing the newcomer.

A few nights later, my brother and sister and I were laughing about Fritz and how he tried to run away from school. Papa overheard us. In a very stern voice he said, "Tomorrow morning I want you kids to go over there, call for Fritz and walk to school with him."

After that, we became good friends. He was a likeable kid and a fast learner. The family bought fresh milk from us, furnished by our cow, Mollie, and also any sour milk we had left over.

But to get back to my story. I had never known Fritz to hop a freight. But one late afternoon, about five o'clock, there was a big commmotion along the tracks just north of Western Avenue. Fritz's father, who worked for the railroad, was walking along the tracks on his way home when he saw people picking up parts of a badly mutilated body and dropping the pieces into a basket.

Mr. Jonas remarked to another worker how glad he was that his son didn't hop freights. When he arrived home Fritz wasn't there. He checked the neighborhood, still not suspecting the body on the tracks could be his son. Late that night, some of Fritz's friends identified the pieces of the body—later confirmed by his grief-stricken father. Fritz was thirteen years old.

It was a terrible shock. I couldn't believe it—not Fritz! Parents re-issued warnings, reminding their kids of what happened to 'that nice young boy'. But, it didn't help. Deaf to the advice, kids continued flipping rides.

Chapter 8

The Neighborhood Circus

"Ruth, Rod, Marge, come on out!" Ida shouted.

When we jumped to run out, Mama got a sour look on her face. "You kids would stand on your head all day if Ida asked you to!" Mama said. Mama was usually right.

"We're gonna put on a circus next week so we've got a lot to do," Ida explained, "we'll charge admission and make a lot of money. We've got to get stuff ready to sell, then we'll plan the side shows and practice for the regular acts."

"First thing we'll do is to get some colored sand and arrange it in bottles," Ida continued. We were all eager to begin.

We had two favorite spots for collecting the colored sand; the limestone cliff across the river and the one on Afton Road near the entrance to the quarry. This day we went out the Afton Road to the quarry entrance - the quarry Ida decided was the perfect setting for directing an opera. While she stood on the floor of the quarry waving her arms, we stood high up the quarry bank on narrow ledges. Our bodies and voices trembled, adding a quavering tone to our operatic renditions.

Using an old tablespoon, I scraped out the various colors putting each color in a separate small paper bag. I collected pink, light green, a darker green, yellow, and white. We each kept our own colors. When we got home we found some small, narrow pill bottles with a thick cork on top. Ida told us to make artistic arrangements by swirling the colors. Before starting their arrangement, some of the girls mixed the colors to get a special color, and others used chalk on the white sand to come up with pastel effects. I just used the colors I had. I wasn't very good at it so I didn't try to swirl it. I put the darkest green on the bottom, added some pink sand and then a layer of lighter green, capping it with the white on top.

"Do you think someone will buy this for two cents?" I asked holding it up.

"Maybe Mama will," Ruth said, in a snotty way.

We talked about the circus plans while we worked. "Can we have a snake show?" Hank Thom asked. Ida, who wasn't scared of anything, was terrified of snakes.

"No, we're not gonna have a snake show," Ida shouted.

"You won't have to do anything with 'em. We'll take care of them," Hank went on.

After a lot of pleading, Ida finally consented and the boys headed for the railroad bank to capture the snakes. In a couple of hours, they found six big snakes and a lot of small ones.

"Let's put the big snakes in separate boxes and give them special names," Jake suggested, "and we'll keep all the small ones in one box." They all agreed it was a good idea, but while Hank was moving one of the big snakes, it bit him in the finger.

It seemed as though everything happened to Hank. When we were picking cherries in their cherry tree, he got a cherry pit in his ear. Another time a pit got up his nostril. I never quite understood how, but I know it was a real hassle to get it out, requiring a visit from the doctor. Then there was the time he stepped on a board and a rusty nail stuck in his foot. He tried to shake off the board but it wouldn't come loose. He reached down to brace the board. That was when another nail pierced his hand.

"Now if he did it to his left hand and foot, everyone would think he'd been crucified," one of the kids said, trying to pretend he didn't feel sorry for him.

Anyway, that night Hank's finger puffed up and turned fiery red. When his mother, who was usually quiet and patient, saw his hand, she shouted, "Get rid of those snakes." Protests that they were needed for the circus fell on deaf ears. They had to go.

"We'll dress up some of the girls like gypsies and that can be the sideshow," Ida decided, relieved not to have to worry about the snakes.

"Now let's make some little scissors. We can sell them for a penny," Ida said getting back to things to sell.

Ruth went in the house and brought out some straight pins and we climbed up the bank to the railroad tracks. We laid the pins on the track, crossing one pin with another. Then we left to wait for a train to run over them and press them together so they'd look like doll scissors.

Someone suggested putting some pennies on the track to get flattened out but nobody had a penny. "Anyway, it doesn't matter because last time we couldn't sell them for two cents," Ida said, "we can make more money with a lemonade stand. But right now it's time to line up the acts and start practicing."

Ida selected girls to be the gypsies and boys to be the clowns. She picked Norma Schumacher to do the Hula, the Shimmy, and the splits—the only one who could really shimmy and shake. Ida chose Maxine Fitch, a natural acrobat, to perform a dance routine and Ruth Thom to read a poem. Then she chose Rod as the announcer. She wasn't sure what to do with Ruth and me. She finally decided that for the opening, Ruth and I would stand on our heads and rest our feet up against Rod.

We began to practice even though Rod wasn't very happy about having to catch our feet and steady them. We tried again and again. We weren't very good but were determined to do well.

We continued to practice with Rod struggling to hold our feet steady, when Ruth made a funny noise, sort of a gaspy laugh. I flopped down on the grass and looked at her. She was upside down, her beet-red face partially covered by her blonde hair, as she wheezed, "I guess Mama was right!"

But, let it be known, Ruth and I weren't the only ones "who would stand on your head all day if Ida asked you to." Others worked just as hard. Kids strung sheets over our clotheslines to form the main tent. Crates and chairs were hauled over for the customers to sit on.

The gypsies' outfits were bold and colorful. With their faces rouged and hair marcelled, they donned dangling earrings, bands of bracelets and chunky beads. Pie plates became their tambourines. They were spectacular as they practiced their dances.

Rod wore a blue serge suit and a top hat. Ruth and I were not very happy in our white blouses and black bloomers, especially as compared to Norma and Maxine's costumes and the gypsies.

The big day finally arrived. Customers came filling up the chairs and crates.

"Good afternoon. Welcome to the all new Monterey Neighborhood Circus," Rod shouted as he held our jiggling feet. He announced the first act and the show started. Ruth and I were through performing so between acts, Ida told us to go through the crowd to sell the colored sand, miniature scissors, and lemonade.

The clowns, dressed mostly like tramps with blackened faces, did a few tricks and mingled with the audience. They scared, yet delighted, the small kids. Some of the mothers felt Norma's act was too risque when she shimmied her heart out to "No One Can Shimmy Like my Sister, Kate." Others clapped enthusiastically. Maxine was the darling of the show with her twirls, cartwheels and back bends.

When the main show was over, Ida began barking the side show, "For just two cents more, you can see the colorful Gypsy side show. Step right over here and see these authentic Gypsy dancers." Ida motioned them to our chicken coop where it would be held. But a problem developed. In order for the gypsies to have room to dance, they had to be down front. So Ida tried to get the patrons to sit on the slanted, slotted roosts. Although the kids scrambled up, the older women complained. They had good reason—not only because it was difficult for some of the older, fatter women to get up there, but because the boards were still covered with whitish speckles.

Ida finally conceded, "All right, we'll let the gypsies perform out in the yard, even though everyone hasn't paid the extra two cents."

Admittedly, it was our best circus. When it was over, we felt let down. All the excitement and anticipation we had enjoyed for weeks was gone. Even so, I had a pleasant reminder of our big circus. On the window sill in the kitchen, stood my artistic creation—a sand bottle.

Chapter 9

Games We Played

"Give 'em to me. They're mine!" I shouted as I grabbed for the bag of marbles.

"I will not. They're mine. I won them fair and square," Jake shouted, holding them away from me.

"You did not. You didn't say anything about playing for keeps," I yelled.

"I always play for keeps and you know it!"

"You better give 'em to me or I'll tell Mama. She'll tell your mother," I threatened. Mama always took my part.

"Might as well give 'em to you or Ma'll grab me by the ear and drag me over to your house and make me say, *"I'm sorry"* to Miss Goody-Goody." He spat out the words, flinging the marbles in the dirt by my feet. The thing Jake hated the most was to have to say "I'm sorry". He'd take a beating before he would say it, and I knew it.

I played marbles with the boys because most of the girls didn't like to play. I prized my marbles and the colorful shooters. I wasn't a very good player, but if I did happen to win, I'd keep the marbles. However when I lost, I screamed and yelled, "We weren't playing for keeps!" It usually worked.

I knew what I was doing wasn't exactly fair, but felt I was pretty smart because I was getting by with it. These thoughts were going through my head as I smugly counted and sorted my ever-increasing supply of marbles, not unlike a miser counting his money.

"Mama, will you make me another marble bag?"

"Another one, Margie?" That meant she would.

Everything was going along fine until my sister, always "Miss Righteous", tattled to Papa.

"That's C-H-E-A-T-I-N-G !" he shouted, drawing out the word to make sure it sunk in.

It did. Papa went with me to make sure I gave back all of my ill-gotten gains. We went to Jake's house last. I held out the bag of marbles, turning my head away from him as I said, "I'm sorry I cheated." Nothing happened. He didn't grab the bag of marbles.

"Take them, Jake, they belong to you," Papa said. I turned to look at Jake. I expected he would be laughing and gloating about getting back his marbles. Instead, his eyes were clouded and sad. He was feeling sorry for me. Papa pushed the bag in Jake's hand and we left.

Strangely enough, I didn't feel sorry for myself. I knew what I did was wrong and that Papa was right. I felt better to be out of the marble racket.

I still played mumbletypeg with the boys. There wasn't much to argue about, either the jackknife stuck or it didn't, as we threw it from various positions. Although, at times, heated discussions decided whether, or not, the knife was high enough off the ground.

During recess and after school, the girls played hopscotch. If we had a sidewalk to play on, we'd outline the squares with chalk, but usually, we played in the dirt using a sharp stick to etch out the outlines for the game. We hopped on one foot, careful not to step on the lines, as we picked up the marker. I always tried to find a piece of glass in a pretty color for my marker—turquoise, bright blue or red. I had the coordination and balance to win at this. I thought it was fun but not very exciting.

One of my favorite games was Jacks which we played by the hour, sometimes on the steps of our back porch using the wood floor to play on; other times (usually) we sat on the cement walk. To play, we threw a small ball in the air, picked up a jack, or jacks, from the surface, then caught the ball when it bounced. We sometimes used a rubber ball, but I preferred a golf ball on a cement surface. If you didn't catch the ball, or if you moved a jack, or didn't pick up the right number of jacks, you lost your turn.

We used from six to ten jacks going through the one's, two's, etc. starting with easy games and working on up to the more difficult. Some of the stunts I remember are *Downs and Ups, Eggs in a Basket, Upcast, Downcast, Hot Potato,* and *Pigs in a Pen.* In Hot Potato, we had to pick up the jacks and catch the ball before it bounced which made it more difficult.

After sitting playing Jacks, we liked to jump rope, sometimes one at a time or in pairs. We enjoyed "1-2-3, O'Leary" - bouncing a ball and lifting our foot over it, or doing other maneuvers, before catching it.

While the girls were busy at their activities, the boys raced around on their home-made scooters with handles for steering. With one foot on the scooter they used the other to propel themselves around the neighborhood, usually at break-neck speeds. They made another contraption for rolling a bicycle tire. They found a narrow board in the scrap pile and nailed another board crosswise along the bottom, then ran up and down the street pushing the bicycle tire. Some were pretty good at it and rolled the tire for several blocks, depending on their skill and the roughness of the street.

Unlike most girls, my sister and I didn't play with dolls very often. Using scraps of material, we occasionally cut clothes for our small celluloid dolls, but didn't sew them. We held the dress together by tying a ribbon around it as a sash. We enjoyed cutting out paper dolls and dressing them in various outfits. They were always better dressed than our regular dolls.

On Saturdays, from early morning to late afternoon, we played "Work-Up" in the street in front of our house. We usually had two players at bat and the rest in various field positions. When a batter made out, the other players would 'move up'. The catcher became the batter, the pitcher was

Rod, Ruth and I with our cousin, Pembroke Pengri, on the banks of Rock River.

catcher, first baseman moved to pitcher, etc. The player who made out had to start over again in left field to work his way back up to bat. (Unless he happened to hear his mother call, which sometimes happened.)

By far my favorite game was "Hide and Seek", which we played in the early evening when it was getting dark. To decide who was going to be "It" for the first time, we went through a rigamarole with "Eenie, Meeny, Miny Mo". However, whoever was "It" had a chance to get out of it. He went to the 'home base tree', crossed his arms over his eyes and leaned against the shaggy bark. The rest gathered around and after some mumbo-jumbo, someone would make a circle on his back and give him a poke. "It" would turn around and try to guess who poked him. If he was right, the one who poked was "it"; if he guessed wrong, he was still "It."

"It" turned back to the tree, eyes covered, as he started to count to one hundred by five's. We'd hear him counting 5-10-15-20, as we raced away to hide. When he reached one hundred, he yelled, "Here I come, ready or not," and started to look for us. When he spotted a player, they raced back to the tree. If the player got there first, he'd yell, "Home free!", but if "It" got there first, the player was "It" and the game started all over.

I tried to find a hiding place where I could spy on "It". I watched and listened for any movement in the shadows. When I thought he was far enough away from the base, I'd run pell-mell in the spine-tingling race to be "FREE".

Games were an important part of our lives. Without adult supervision, we found plenty to do. We ran, jumped, laughed, screamed and shouted as we sharpened our skills, competing with one another. Along the way, we learned to abide by the rules of the game and to play fair—sometimes with difficulty.

Chapter 10

City Conveniences

The sickening stench, the pesky flies, the harshness of the page from the Sears, Roebuck catalog, and, in the winter, having to bundle up, dreading the thought of sitting and shivering on the cold, clammy seat. That's how I remember our outside toilet.

Although most of the remaining privies in our neighborhood were two-holers, ours was a three-seater with a small, a medium, and a large hole to accommodate various-sized buttocks. Knotholes in the wide boards provided ventilation, along with a small crescent-shape opening on the upper side of one wall. This distinguishing feature is how you could tell a backhouse from a small tool shed.

Somehow, no matter how uncomfortable I was, I took time to thumb through what was left of the Sears catalog. As I turned the pages, I dreamed of getting some of the merchandise pictured—a pale blue, voile dress, black patent slippers, or a pair of roller skates. But in the end, the harshness of the torn catalog page quickly brought me back to reality, reminding me of a friend's visit to a girl's house who had inside plumbing. My friend was so impressed with the softness of the toilet tissue, that she rolled off several arm-lengths and stuffed it in one bloomer leg, then rolled off more for the other leg. As she walked back in the living room, the tissue made a rustling sound attracting the attention of the girl's mother. My red-faced friend said, " I have to go home now,". She swish-swished her way out as fast as she could. Later she explained,

"But, y'know, they didn't even have a Sears Roebuck catalog in there."

At our house, near the back porch along with the privy, was a pump. We had no running water. Ruth, Rod and I pumped the water and did the running, especially on Monday, wash days, and on Saturdays for our baths. We poured the water in the reservoir on the side of our big kitchen stove where it was heated by the fire, providing us with a good supply of hot water. On Saturdays, Mama hauled out her square metal laundry tub and placed it near the stove. A kitchen chair was moved next to the tub for towels, soap and underwear. Mama put on a dark print coverall apron, rolled up her sleeves and ladled the water from the reservoir to fill up the tub. My sister was the oldest so she was first, then my brother and finally me. Mama didn't change the water for each bath. She just kept adding to it to keep it warm and for rinsing.

One morning after Mama scrubbed me, my skin smarted from the harsh soap and rough washcloth. As I grabbed a towel. I turned around and noticed some groceries on the kitchen table. Sometimes when Mama needed groceries, she called the store, ordered what she needed, and in a short time they were delivered to the house.

"When did the groceries come?" I asked my brother who was coloring at the kitchen table.

"The grocery boy just brought them and he got a peek at your birthmark," Rod gleefully informed me.

His words pierced me like a hot iron. I felt my neck heat up, then spread up to my cheeks. I started to cry, ashamed that someone had seen the unsightly red mark on my left buttock.

"If we just had city water and a bath, this wouldn't have happened," I sobbed. Mama tried to console me as she started emptying the water.

"Don't worry about it, he probably didn't even see you. But, I'll be glad too when we get hooked up to city water."

She explained that the city had installed sewer and water lines down our street but our landlord decided not to hook up with it. What really rankled Mama was that Papa had allowed the landlord to "top off" the privy just before the ordinance went into effect.

"But he can't hold off much longer because there's a ruling that states anyone who needs a new toilet has to convert to an indoor one. And, you know ours is just about full," she said, trying to reassure me.

Her words didn't help. I felt a wave of embarrassment surge through me as I thought of facing the good-looking grocery boy who was a grade ahead of me in school. During the next few weeks, whenever I saw him, I'd run and hide. If I saw him coming down the street, I crossed to the other side and I refused to go to the store no matter what Mama said.

The subject of city conveniences didn't come up again until a few days before Halloween. This was the time the remaining outhouses received a lot of attention from pranksters. But for some reason, ours seemed to enjoy an immunity.

"I wish someone would tip over our privy, then the landlord would have to install city plumbing," Mama said to Papa. Her voice, usually soft and low, was loud and high-pitched.

He pooh-poohed the idea.

"No one's going to touch it, Carrie. Everyone likes us around here."

"But Bill, it's wobbly and it's almost full. He's going to have to do it sooner or later because you know it's illegal to dig another one," Mama persisted.

Papa grabbed his newspaper and buried his face in it. From long experience, Mama knew that when the newspaper went up, it was akin to hanging out a "Do Not Disturb" sign.

Although Papa dismissed the conversation, Mama had not. The next morning when Mama was washing dishes, she saw Martha, our next door neighbor, outside in the yard. Mama wiped her hands, took off her apron and met up with Martha by the lilac bushes. It wasn't long before Mama brought up the discussion of the previous night.

"It's certainly time you had city water, you sure pay enough rent," Martha sympathized. They were one of the first households on the block to convert. The conversation continued as they hashed over the many reasons for getting rid of the unsightly, unsafe and unsanitary outhouse.

"I feel like pushing it over myself," Mama grumbled.

"I'll help you, Carrie," Martha whispered as she leaned closer to Mama. Although she spoke softly, she was emphatic.

Mama was taken aback. "Martha, what are you saying?" She couldn't believe the words coming from this sedate, dignified, maiden lady.

Mama laughed at the absurdity of the idea, but soon conceded, "It's so wobbly, it wouldn't take much to push it over. I think we could do it."

"Let's do it on Halloween night," Martha said.

The next day Mama and Martha, giggling like schoolgirls, planned the demise of the privy, "Let's meet by the outhouse. We'll wait until ten o'clock in case some hoodlums decide to push it over," Mama said, "also, Bill and the kids will be in bed."

"Don't go inside or someone might come along and push it over, with you in it, like they did to Katie last year," Martha said with a grin on her face.

They laughed as they recalled how Katie's backhouse was always a target on Halloween night which made her decide to guard against vandals by sitting in it. The culprits came and attacked from the rear. Over it went with Katie penned in it.

"She was lucky Gussie from next door heard her calls or she would have been stuck in there all night. We don't want anything like that to happen to us," Martha chuckled.

Although they were laughing about their planned Halloween mission, both were inwardly hoping someone else would do the dirty work for them. However at ten o'clock, when Mama looked out, the toilet was still standing. She drew a deep breath and slipped out the back door. Martha was waiting for her.

They made an unlikely pair for any wrong-doing; Mama in her prim, high-neck blouse and full, pleated skirt that just touched the top of her button shoes and Martha in a navy serge dress covered with an apron, and a fringed scarf over her shoulders.

After a quiet greeting they set right to work. They decided to try to dislodge it from the front. They leaned on the outhouse, pushing against it with all their might. Time after time, they pushed and shoved. It didn't budge. They tried the same tactics on one side. Then the other side. That didn't work either.

"It's sturdier than I thought," Mama whispered.

"Let's each get a clothes pole and push on the roof from the back," Martha suggested.

"That might work," Mama agreed. They crept quietly to the back yard which was right under Papa's window and picked out a long, sturdy pole. As they started back for the privy, they heard noises from the street.

"What's that? Who's coming?" Mama asked in a hushed voice. They dropped the clothes poles and ran for cover in the bushes. The women hid in the shadows, trembling at the thought of being caught red-handed, as the noises became louder. They watched as three men shuffled unsteadily past the front of the house, turn the corner and disappear under the arch.

"Do you think we ought to give up?" Martha asked.

"No. They're gone, let's try again," Mama replied.

After retrieving the poles, they braced them in position under the overhang of the roof. Martha whispered, "One - Two - Three, PUSH." They pushed with all their strength. Nothing happened. They tried again.

"I think it's beginning to loosen up. I felt it start to give," Mama said.

"Let's rest a minute and then give it another try. I'm sure we can do it," Martha whispered.

After catching their breath, they readjusted the poles. "One - Two - Three, SHOVE!" The women gave a mighty heave.

The toilet slowly gave way. Over it went - taking Mama and Martha, still clinging to the poles, with it. The women looked down at the messy pit below as they dangled on the poles.

"Oh dear!" cried Martha.

"Shh," squeaked Mama, "Don't wake up Bill."

Mama, whose pole was stuck closest to the edge of the big hole, pushed off with a mighty effort. One foot landed on solid ground, the other on the rim of the pit as she rolled on the ground. She quickly got up, grabbed Martha pulling her, and the pole, to safety.

"Whew, that was close. Let's get out of here," Martha coughed, holding her nose. Each raced for the security of her home.

The next morning Papa started down the porch steps going out for his morning constitutional... a trip to the privy. "CARRIE, CARRIE, someone pushed over our privy," he shouted. "Who would do that?" While he speculated on who-dun-it, Mama squirmed uneasily in her chair. (He never did find out. Besides, I doubt if he would have believed it.)

"C'mon Carrie, we have to put it up again so we can use it," Papa said, helping Mama up off the chair.

Mama learned that the three-holer was even harder to put up than it was to push over. While Mama and Papa struggled with it, Martha strolled over, self-composed and dignified.

"Carrie, what happened?" she asked, sounding as innocent as a child. Papa was much too busy working and cussing to notice the exchange of glances and sly grins.

After an hour, even though the outhouse was back in place, Mama and Martha's unlikely prank got results. Someone (probably Martha) notified the City; the City notified the landlord; the landlord notified Mama and Papa, "I will be installing city plumbing at your home within thirty days."

Mama's eyes shined brightly as we discussed the good news at the supper table. "Oh good. Now we don't have to take our baths in the kitchen and have people walk in on us!" I said, clapping my hands.

"Oh, Margie, I meant to tell you. The grocery boy didn't really come in the kitchen that day. He handed me the groceries at the door," Rod confessed with a big grin.

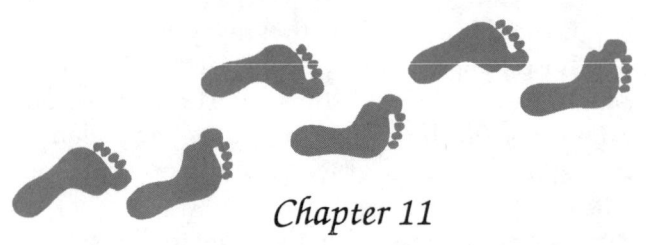

Chapter 11

Rainy Days

Rain drops tap, tap, tapping on the window panes bid us,"Come play!"

Eagerly we accepted the invitation, rushing out to greet the summer rain. It beckoned us to play, gently patting our upturned faces as we danced with easy movements around the yard, arms outstretched - not unlike pagans worshipping the Rain God.

But before long, our rowdy instinct took over. Rod, Ruth and I, along with our neighborhood friends, frolicked and slid in the wet grass. We stomped our bare feet in puddle after puddle, trying to be the one who could splash the highest and get our clothes the muddiest. I squished my feet in the soft, warm mud, watched as it oozed up between my toes, filling me with shivers of delight.

We sat in the ditch by the side of our dirt street where a stream of water was flowing and threw twigs in it. We made grooves in the mud to direct it's flow and built a dam so we could sail makeshift boats. We dug shallow holes and watched the rain splotch in to form puddles.

Then, in the midst of our fun, the rain stopped. Our stream disappeared.

"Shucks, the rain stopped and its spoiling all our fun! What'll we do?" a playmate asked.

Someone remembered that part way up the hill the neighbors had a huge rain barrel placed under the gutters to catch the rain water. All of us had rain barrels but not in the right location to flow into the ditch.

"It'll be full by now. Let's dump old Ichabod's barrel!" someone shouted.

In our eagerness to get water, we forgot how scared we were of this neighbor with wild bushy hair, overly long arms that swung disjointedly as he loped along, his dark eyes peering from deep, dark sockets. Up the hill we charged.

We ran around to the side of the run-down stone house and grouped around the wooden barrel. We pushed, but it didn't budge. We pushed again, and yet again. Finally, with a mighty heave-ho, we tipped the heavy barrel. The water flowed - but we didn't get to enjoy it.

Suddenly, six foot, four Ichabod ran around the corner of the house and saw what we had done. He let out an unearthly, belligerent bellow that sent us flying down the hill scared out of our wits. His gangling body, all arms and legs, was gaining on us as we raced down the gravel hill. As he came closer, his bellowing and shouting became louder and louder.

When we reached the foot of the hill, we made a wild dash for the front door of our house, startling Mama as we bumped her as we dripped through the house and raced out the back door - just as Ichabod pushed open the front door.

"Your kids dumped over our rain barrel," we heard him scream to Mama as we raced to the chicken coop and huddled in one corner as my brother lowered the poop-speckled, canvas curtain.

I could imagine how frightened Mama was with Ichabod's long arms swinging menacingly over her head, his wild eyes scanning the rooms, his face gaunt and distorted with anger. Nevertheless, we counted on her to calm him down, or at least to slow him down.

But not for long. We heard the back door slam and his footsteps coming toward the chicken coop.

"Everyone sit still. Don't even breathe," Ruth cautioned.

"But I have to sneeze," Norma whispered.

"Don't you dare, he'll kill us!"

Norma pressed her finger against her upper lip and held

her breath as we trembled quietly on the roost, flocked together, squeezing hard against the wall. The door squeaked open. His footsteps came closer. We heard him grab the canvas curtain on the far end of the coop. Quickly, he shoved it up. We could see the outline of his huge head as he peered inside the dark roost. We sat frozen with fear. The curtain dropped. We heard his footsteps going away.

A few moments later, he came back. He pushed the door open, shuffled around, then stopped, as though listening for a sound. Then the door slammed shut. We heard him head towards the barn.

We sat there shaking, not making a sound, for a long time—until Mama came out looking for us. Our relief at seeing Mama didn't last long; our danger was not over. We had forgotten that Mama had the same reverence for rain water that Catholics have for Holy Water.

"That was a mean thing to do! They needed that water for baths and laundry. Shame on you, shame on you," she screamed, scornfully pointing her left forefinger at us while stroking it with the right forefinger. I cringed.

She turned to our friends, "Go home right now! I'll talk to your mothers later!" They fled quickly, glad to get away.

She then turned her attention to Rod, Ruth and I.

"You kids are going to fill up that rain barrel before you get any supper," she yelled, her eyes blazing. I had never seen her so angry.

We filled pails with water from our rain barrels, but before we would start up the hill, we made sure that Mama went ahead to make peace with our neighbor.

Up and down, back and forth, trip after trip, we went, Rod, Ruth and I tugging and sloshing the heavy buckets.

Looking up I thought I saw the shape of the Rain God hiding in a cloud looking down on our unhappy bucket brigade. His head seemed to shake as he said, "I hope they learned when I no longer want to play, it's time for them to stop too. And they must always respect other people's property."

At least that's what I thought I heard.

Chapter 12

Looking Out For One Another

Y ou children look out for one another!"

That's what Mama always said when we were going out to play. She had this firm belief that as long as the three of us were together, we would be safe. This conviction of our well-being was deepened because we were usually joined by two other families; the Thoms and Hubers—plus the fact that we were careful not to tell her about any of our hair-raising antics.

This gave my sister and brother and me all the leeway we needed to enjoy to the hilt our summer days with Ida and our friends.

It was a mid-week morning. All days sort of ran together during the summer so I was never sure of the exact day of the week. We were eating breakfast at the kitchen table when we heard a familiar call,

"Ruth, Rod, Marge, come on out!" Ida yelled.

"C'mon, hurry up!" Ida bellowed impatiently.

We slurped down the rest of our oatmeal and milk and rushed out the door where Ida greeted us, "My Pa said they're gonna dump watermelons at the Five Points this morning."

Mama followed us out to the back porch, calling out those familiar words, "You children look out for one another, do you hear?" Before this day was over, I would remember Mama's parting words.

Rod grabbed our red, iron wagon and the Thom kids joined us as we all started up Center Avenue for the Five Points, the hub of railroad activity in Janesville.

When the fruit loaded in a railway car became ripe before reaching its destination, the railroad men dumped it at the Five Points crossing for folks to pick up.

Word spread quickly People of all ages, mostly women and children carrying baskets and grocery bags, crowded by the car. We watched eagerly as the door of the freight car opened and the watermelons rolled onto the ground. We darted in to pick out the best melons and load them in the wagon. When the wagon was full, we each grabbed a big melon or a couple of small ones and started back down Center Avenue with Rod managing the overloaded wagon. We walked down the hill until we reached the Rock River near the Monterey Bridge and dumped the melons in the grass near the river bank.

We had no knife to cut them, so we threw them on the ground, watching them break into big chunks. We scrambled for the pieces, burying our faces in the juicy melon. I felt the sticky juice smearing my chin, nose and cheeks, as it dripped on my white blouse and skirt. I just kept eating and eating.

Even though we ate like slobbering pigs, there was one thing we were careful about. We knew we must not swallow any of the watermelon seeds. If we did, a melon would grow in our stomach. We knew this was true. We had seen it happen to several women in our neighborhood. As we spit out the seeds, they flew in all directions as we continued to wolf down the tasty melons. Finally, we reached a point when we couldn't eat another bite. "Let's go swimming", someone suggested. We would soon learn this was not a good idea.

We usually swam at The Island downstream past the Woolen Mill because it was not as deep and had less of a current. But today, we joined the others, wading into the river with all our clothes on. Rod, Ruth and me, along with some of the other kids, stayed in the shallow water near the shore, splashing the cold water on our hot, dirty faces and on one another. My sister cupped her hands spraying me with a shower of water. I turned my back, scooping water at her with all my might, like a dog digging a hole.

The water spattered in all directions, glistening in the bright sun as we laughed and shouted at one another.

It seemed we had only been in the water a short time when I looked up and saw Walter Thom, the oldest brother of our friends, jump off the abutment where he was fishing and race towards us, splashing water as high as his head as he came nearer. He had a worried look on his face as he hurried our way. I wondered what was the matter.

As soon as he got near, he quickly bent down, stretched his arms into the river and swooped up a limp, lifeless form.

"Is it Rodney?" someone asked, "Is he dead?"

I didn't believe it could be Rod. He was wading right next to me in water barely up to our knees. I looked around but couldn't find him.

I watched Walt tip the body upside down and pound his back.

Suddenly, I knew it had to be Rod even though it didn't look like him. His face was blue and his blonde hair, matted flat to his head, looked black. My heart thumped like it was trying to jump out of my body. I grabbed my sister's arm and held on to her.

"Oh, I hope he doesn't die," I cried, tears rolling down my cheeks. I thought of Mama's words, "Look out for one another."

How could this happen? What would she say?

Walter again pounded my brother's limp form. Water ran out of his mouth. He coughed. Still holding him upside down, Walter slapped his back again. We heard a gurgle and a gasp. We followed Walter as he carried Rod to shore, putting him down on the grass.

"He should be all right," Walt mumbled as he trudged off to get back to his fishing.

Rod held his knees to his chest but that didn't stop his whole body from shaking and twitching. Purple bumps covered his skin and his lips were a purplish blue. He continued to shake as Ida wrapped a dry shirt over his shoulders. Other kids found clothing to cover Rod as he continued shivering, his teeth chattering.

"Can you breathe?" I asked as I rubbed his goose-bumped arms, "What happened?" His glassy eyes looked at me.

"I got a cramp and doubled up. I could hear everybody talking and laughing but I couldn't move," Rod wheezed as his teeth kept making a funny noise, "I wondered why no one saw me."

"It's lucky Walt saw you floating face down," someone said.

Yeah, lucky someone was looking out for him,—it sure wasn't me. Mama would never forgive us if anything happened to Rod. He was always her favorite.

When Rod finally stopped shaking and his color returned, my sister and I put him in the wagon, along with the few remaining watermelons, and pulled him home.

"How nice of you girls to give Rodney a ride in the wagon," Mama said, not noticing he was still a little blue, "and what

Rod takes our Jersey cow, Mollie, out to graze.

nice melons!"

We didn't say anything to Mama about Rod's brush with death. We were afraid it might change her belief that as long as we were together, nothing would happen to us.

But that night when I crawled into bed I thought of what happened. Now I understood Mama's words of caution. What she meant—what she was trying to tell us. I wondered why it took Rod's near drowning to make her words sink in. My body twitched and I started to cry.

Rod was my favorite too!

Chapter 13

Crazy Daisy

The big black dog we called Happy came bounding up the steps of our back porch where Rod and I were playing jacks. He rubbed his big body against us pushing us from side to side. The jacks scattered all over the porch as his tail whacked the floor in a steady beat. He pushed his head under my arm, then nuzzled Rod.

"He's really glad to see us," Rod said, "I sure wish we could keep him."

The friendly dog visited us almost daily but we knew he had an owner who really cared for him as he was well fed, had a shiny coat of fur and even a collar.

As we continued to pet him and wrestle with him, Rod said, "Look, Margie, he has a note on his collar."

"I'll bet the owner is mad at us for taking her dog away," I said. "But read it, read it," I said impatiently.

Rod carefully unfolded the note and read it aloud, "I know you love my dog as much as I do and I'm glad he has someone else to care for him. I would like to meet you. Please come to my house at three o'clock Saturday." Signed, Daisy. And it gave the address.

When Saturday came, Rod and I walked up to the door of a big cream colored, brick mansion and timidly raised the brass knocker.

The door opened and a small, pleasant woman welcomed us. "My sister-in-law, Daisy, is expecting you," she said quietly. She turned and rapped loudly on a door off the dining room.

After pounding several times, the door opened. Out burst a large woman with hair piled wildly and loosely on top of her head, "I'M HARD OF HEARING," she shouted. I guess she thought we were too. "I'LL CALL BLACKIE IN TO SEE YOU."

When she opened the door, the dog bounced in, jumped on Rod and me, his tail going a mile a minute.

"We call him Happy, because he's such a happy dog," I explained.

Daisy smiled although I'm not sure she could hear me. Blackie's actions seemed to assure her that we were indeed the rightful recipients of her note. She seemed grateful, not at all jealous, because she had to share his affection.

"Let's go back in my room. I was hoping you would come so I baked some sugar cookies for you," she said a little more softly. Her big black eyes, sunken deep in the sockets, darted from Rod to Blackie and me in a continuous circuit.

We followed her into a dark room. When my eyes adjusted to the dimness, I saw I had to be careful where I walked because the floor was cluttered with newspapers and magazines. Other papers were stacked in piles, dozens of them, all over the room. Clothes and towels were strung over the chairs. Then I realized why it was so dark—the windows were boarded up.

"Do you think she wants to get rid of Blackie—that she wants to give him to us?" Rod whispered uneasily when she went to get the cookies. I shrugged my shoulders but didn't answer. I didn't need to be afraid she would hear us but I didn't feel like talking. I was scared.

She came back with the cookies heaped on a discolored pie plate. We helped ourselves and shared them with "Blackie" who romped all over us, happy we were there.

She urged us to have more. The story of Gretel and Hansel with the Witch came to mind. I was anxious to get out.

"We have to go home now or Mama will be worried," I said.

She sighed. "You are wonderful children to love Blackie the

way you do. Let's continue to share him and please write me a note once in a while and tell me of your adventures with him. You can attach them to his collar," she said as we got up to leave.

At the door, she grabbed me. Her long bony fingers dug into my arm holding me firmly. "I'm very lonesome here. Do come see me again. "When we assured her we would, she let go of my arm.

Rod and I were glad to get outside and in the sunshine.

We ran most of the way home which was about a mile away.

"She was a little different, wasn't she?" Rod gasped.

"Yeah, scary but sort of nice. She was especially nice about Blackie, as she calls him, spending so much time with us," I replied.

When we got home, we rushed in to tell Mama and Papa about our visit.

"Oh, that must be 'Crazy Daisy'," Papa said, obviously amused at the idea. "She comes from a fine family but is slightly off her rocker. If her sister-in-law didn't take care of her, she would have to go to the County Insane Asylum." he explained.

"What's an asylum?" I asked.

"It's a place where they send people who are mentally incompetent, who can't take care of themselves and who don't have anyone to care for them," he replied.

"It must be awful," Rod said, his eyes wide with concern.

Papa nodded his head, "It is bad. You kids keep on writing notes to Daisy and it's all right to visit her. She'll be glad to see you," he said.

We continued to write notes back and forth. A few weeks later, she invited us to come see her the following Saturday and she would have cookies for us. This time we took our older sister along. The nice lady opened the door and said sadly, "I know Daisy invited you to come but she isn't able to receive visitors today. She asked me to give you this bag of cookies."

We could hear a wailing in the background and someone pounding.

"Thank you, and tell Miss Daisy thanks too," I said as we quickly took the cookies and left.

We were quiet on the way home. We didn't want to believe that our new friend could act like that. That night we talked to Papa about it.

"Just think of what her sister-in-law goes through every day just to keep her out of the asylum," he said sadly.

"What makes her like that?" Ruth asked.

Papa shook his head, "No one really knows what causes them to be irrational. There must be a hundred people in the County Asylum now and many more are sent to Mendota in Madison."

"There's a big fellow, named Billie, who lives near the Fourth Ward Park that the kids say is crazy. He lives with his mother," Rod said.

"Yeah, and whenever he's out in the yard the big boys make faces at him and throw sticks at him until he gets mad and chases them," Ruth said.

"Yeah, and then the mother, who is real small, runs down the sidewalk after him. She talks to him, tries to calm him down and get him back home," Rod added.

"Have you told your teacher about this?" Papa asked. He was obviously quite upset. "Do you kids realize how difficult it is for his mother to take care of him? Don't you know it's mean of the kids to tease him? Do they realize they're making it that much harder for the mother?"

We hadn't really thought about it before.

"One day Billie picked up a stick and chased one of the boys who was teasing him. The boy's father called the police and said he should be put away," Ruth said.

"The tormentor is the one who should be put away," Papa said angrily. "If those kids don't stop aggravating him, the mother won't be able to handle him and will have to put him in the insane asylum." Now Papa was really upset.

We never thought much about it before but now we were concerned too.

That night Papa wrote a long letter to the school principal,

Miss Atwood, that started out, "It has come to my attention ". telling about what was happening.

We delivered it the next morning. That same day Miss Atwood visited every classroom. Her eyes blazed as she started out, "It has come to my attention". She went on to explain that some people are afflicted with mental problems, describing their behaviour. She told of the difficulty of caring for them. She then went into a graphic description of insane asylums and what happened to the people who were sent there.

"That's what happens to the mentally sick if they can't be cared for at home." She looked from face to face. "I expect you boys and girls to treat these unfortunate people the way you would want to be treated—and don't create any more problems for their caretakers!" She shouted.

The girls brushed back tears during the fiery speech. The big boys, the culprits, hung their heads in shame.

Miss Atwood made her point. The kids understood. That problem was settled once and for all and Billie continued to live at home peacefully with no one bothering him.

Daisy continued to write us notes sending them on the collar of our mutual friend. Either Rod or I answered them. We'd think of something funny to tell her about Blackie and then we'd tell her what a fine dog he was and thank her for taking such good care of him.

One day she wrote, "I would like to see you again but I have not been feeling well."

"She doesn't know when she might have another spell," Papa explained.

Rod and I weren't disappointed. Much as we enjoyed the cookies, we preferred to visit with Daisy by placing messages on Blackie's collar.

Chapter 14

School Days

"Mama, can I please go to school today? Please?"

For as long as I remember, I wanted to go to school. Maybe it was because I missed Ruth and Rod when they went to school leaving me behind, but I'd like to think it was because I was anxious to learn about everything. I did learn to read early, probably because Ruth liked to play teacher and because I thought if I could read I could go to school.

Well, it did happen that once I could read, I was allowed to go to school. Douglas school was a big square cement building on the corner of Linn St. and Galena. It was quite barren with no bushes or trees, just a gravelly, sandy play area surrounding the two-story building.

The floors were wood, our small desks had a top that lifted up, the front of each desk formed the seat for the one in front. A ridge on the top of each well-worn desk kept our pencil from rolling down the slanted surface. It also had a hole for our ink well, which we needed for dipping our pens. The teacher sat behind a big desk that held an impressive globe and many books. The blackboard covered the wall space on the front and side of the room where there was also a roller holding a map that the teacher pulled down, like a window shade, when teaching geography.

Douglas, an elementary school, had grades one through six. Each grade was divided into "A" and "B"; 1A and 1B, 2A and 2B, etc. Because of these divisions, one class graduated from high school in January and one in June. (Basketball coaches sometimes lost half their players in the middle of the season.)

At our school, we had two grades, with four classes, in each classroom. While three groups worked on assignments, the teacher taught the fourth class. With this arrangement, I found, after doing my work, I could listen in on what was going on in the next class. When the teacher learned I understood the lessons and was able to do the work, she moved me ahead a half-grade. I kept skipping a half grade at a time until I caught up with Rod, who was a year and a half older. This is probably why many students who attended schools with several grades in one classroom or a one room schoolhouse, graduated at a younger age.

The Principal was Miss Abbie Atwood, a friend of the family. She was strict, but kind. Everyone respected her, even the kids who didn't like school. All of the teachers were single women. When a teacher got married, she was replaced.

Parents believed the teachers were always right—they stood firmly behind them. The principal also backed up the teachers. When a teacher punished a student at school, the parents got in their licks when the kid got home.

We often went to great pains to keep our parents from knowing everything that happened at school. One day Miss Atwood came in and asked our teacher to come to the office. As she went out, with her hand on the doorknob, she turned to the class and said, "I expect you to behave while I'm gone, just as though I were here." It was a rare occasion not to have the teacher in the room.

As soon as the door closed, the class exploded. Kids started running around, pell mell. One boy grabbed the teacher's long, wooden pointer. He climbed on her chair swinging it and hitting anyone who came near. An eraser fight erupted with boys lined up in front of the blackboards, slinging the missiles through the air with great speed causing everyone to duck and cover their faces. I sat at my desk for a while, then started running around with the rest of the kids, up and down the aisles, even though I knew I shouldn't.

"Here she comes!" shouted the girl guarding the door. The

The Douglas school was on the corner of Linn and Racine Streets. It was torn down and is now the site of a Fire Station.

kids quickly picked up the erasers and put them back. The boy with the pointer put it back and other kids picked up papers off the floor. As I ran to get in my seat, I slipped on a piece of paper. My cheek smacked the corner of my desk. I held back the tears. I felt blood trickling down my cheek. I held my handkerchief over it. My cheek throbbed. I sat there for two hours until school was out.

I hurried home still holding the hankie to my face. As soon as I saw Mama, I started to cry, tears streaked down my face.

"I fell on the way home and cut my cheek," I lied, as I kept on sobbing. Mama believed me and dressed the wound—but I still have the scar to remind me of my disobedience and dishonesty.

The teachers all seemed to enjoy holidays. To celebrate Valentine's Day we made valentines out of construction paper, scraps of wallpaper, or whatever we could find. We put them in a big cardboard box covered with red tissue paper dotted with white and red hearts. On the big day, the teacher opened the box and took them out one by one. As she called our name, we went forward to get our valentine. I worried that I wouldn't get very many, but I always did. Everyone got at least one because the teacher made one for each of us.

The first Thanksgiving celebration became more vivid as we reenacted the occasion dressed as pilgrims and Indians. On Thanksgiving Day, before cutting the turkey, Rod, Ruth and I donned our costumes to recite the lines we learned in school.

The Christmas program was the one we spent the most time on as we performed before relatives and friends. We sang Christmas carols and put on little skits—one favorite was about the first Christmas tree. For the finale, Baby Jesus was in the manger in the middle of the stage flanked by Mary and Joseph. When the light from the star beamed on the Nativity Scene, it signalled for all the shepherds and angels to come forth from all corners of the room to assemble around the Christ child. When we were all in place, everyone sang Silent Night.

Soon we heard the sound of sleigh bells, faintly at first, then louder. We screamed and shouted our greetings as jolly Santa, with his pack on his back, " Ho, Hoed" his way in, yelling "Merry Christmas to all!" He arrived with a candy cane for all the good little boys and girls. The kids all loved it. It also marked the beginning of our holiday recess—we knew it was none too soon for the nerve-racked teachers.

Once I could read, I liked to be alone with my book. No distractions, just me, feeling close to the people in the book, carried away with their every action or emotion. I often sat on the stairway landing to read, while later on, I'd take my book and climb up the railroad bank and walk along the path until I came to a favorite reading place, a flat rock surrounded by bushes. I'd climb in there, happy that no one would interrupt me with, "You don't have enough light to read there" or "Margie, I want you to run to the store for me."

One afternoon when we were back in school following the

holiday vacation, a friend told me, "I think Steve likes you." I tried to pretend I didn't care but the color in my cheeks gave me away. A short time later, Steve passed me a note. It was the first note I ever got from a boy. I was surprised, and pleased. I quickly put it in my pocket so the teacher wouldn't see it. The teacher had a habit of intercepting notes and reading them aloud to the class. She could take a simple message like "Will you wait for me and I'll walk home with you," into a love story—much to the embarrassment of both the writer and receiver. Steve kept motioning for me to read it but I ignored him. Besides, I wanted to be alone when I read it—my first missile from a boy. I ran all the way home, not even waiting to walk with my friends. Usually walking to and from school was a big deal as we laughed, talked and shared experiences—but today I wanted to be alone. I rushed in the house, took off my coat and ran for the stairway. I sat on the landing and opened the note carefully. Eagerly I read the scrawled message, "Will you lend me a pencil?"

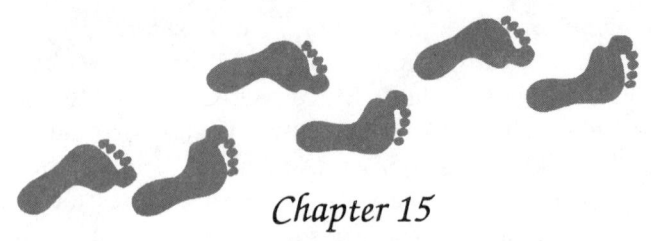

Chapter 15

The Black Pearl Ring

"A new girl is joining our class tomorrow and I expect each one of you to make her feel welcome," our pretty third grade teacher, Miss Sheridan, told us just before we lined up to leave for the day.

The next morning I spotted our new classmate standing alone in the dark entrance above the steps, hunched against the door. Just as I was going to join her, the bell rang and we all went inside.

"This is Violet Buss who has moved to Janesville from Decatur, Iowa." As she introduced the newcomer, Miss Sheridan's soft eyes moved from one face to another—a gentle reminder of her announcement the day before.

Violet's cheeks flushed. With head down and shoulders pulled up, she shyly edged her way to her desk. She was small and pretty with dark wavy hair. She looks nice, I thought.

That afternoon at recess I asked Violet if she wanted to go down by the river with us after school and look for pearls. "I can't go," she said quickly, drawing away from me.

"Are you scared to?", I asked.

"No, but my mother won't let me," she said.

"I'll go home with you and ask her," I suggested.

Although her mother approved, Violet still hung back, probably trying to think of some other excuses. But, I persisted almost dragging her to get her started. We were soon joined by my brother, Rod, and a couple of the Thom kids.

When we reached the old Bulkhead with the water gushing

noisily underneath, Violet grabbed my arm and wouldn't let go until we got across.

We then walked single file along the slippery, narrow path lined with overgrown bushes and trees. Violet stumbled as the toe of her shoe caught on a tree root but she didn't fall because Rod grabbed her. When I brushed up against a willow branch, I was careful to hold it so the branch didn't swing back and sting her face.

Soon we came to a large pile of clams. We didn't know who had dug them or who they belonged to. We thought they were probably for a button factory that made pearl buttons from clam shells, but it didn't make any difference to us.

We sat down around the pile of gray, mucky shells and I showed Violet how to pry them open and where to look for the pearls. But when I tried to hand her a clam, she quickly moved her delicate, white hands behind her back. I forgot about her for a while as the rest of us went to work on the clams. I found a small white pearl, the size of a BB shot. I shoved the grayish muscle to one side and proudly showed Violet the pearl.

After watching us for a while, Violet finally got the courage to try it. On about the third clam, she found a round, black pearl which she brought over for me to see.

"I never saw one that color before - it's beautiful! We've just found white ones," I told her as the others came to admire it. We were excited and happy for her. She was happy too.

My brother and I often found small pearls which we carelessly put in our marble bags. They would somehow disappear and we couldn't find them again. With Violet it was different. She took her pearl home and her mother carefully put it away. Several months went by and Violet and I became good friends. I had forgotten about the black pearl until I went to Violet's birthday party. When it was time to open presents, she unwrapped a small box and slipped a ring on her finger holding it up for all to see, not unlike a young woman showing off her engagement ring.

I stared at the black pearl set in a gold band. The pearl

glowed, elegant and pure. It was the most beautiful ring I had ever seen.

I felt my face getting red, my stomach queazy. It just wasn't fair. I remembered how I practically dragged her down there. Why should she have a ring when I don't? I couldn't understand what was going on. I was happy for her when she found the pearl, why did I feel this way now? It was my first experience with jealousy.

As soon as I could get away from the party, I ran all the way home.

"Mama, Mama, Violet's mother had her pearl set in a pretty ring," I blurted out breathlessly.

"Well, isn't that nice," she responded as she continued kneading the bread dough, pushing back a lock of hair with the back of her flour-covered hand.

> I wondered why she didn't know how I felt. I wanted to ask her why she didn't have a ring made for me - but I didn't. In our reserved household we didn't express our feelings. Even by third grade I had learned to hide mine. Why couldn't I say, "Violet's mother had the black pearl she found set in a beautiful ring and I'm jealous."

I ran up the railroad bank behind our house and sat down on a rock behind a clump of bushes. I was angry at mother. I was even angry at lovely Miss Sheridan blaming her for telling us to be nice to Violet. But, in the end, I blamed Violet—even though I knew she hadn't done anything wrong. I couldn't accept how I felt as being my fault. I didn't know how to deal with it.

After that I didn't play with Violet. I couldn't be her friend. I avoided her. She never knew why. When school was out, her family moved back to Decatur. I never saw her or heard from her again. But, I've often thought about her.

Chapter 16

Douglas Playground

Usually we looked to Ida to decide what we would do, but part of the time during the summer we learned about organized play at the Douglas School playground, where a time schedule was set up for softball, volleyball, track, games, stunt nights and craft. Unwittingly, Margie the Tomboy, who was reluctant to stop playing sports to work on crafts, learned an important lesson.

The program at the elementary schools was supervised by two college students, a woman and a man. Over the years, these special leaders at Douglas school included Carlie Palmer, Roland Gridley, Bill Austin, Al Croft, Jane Gage, Anne Palmer and Dorothy Buss.

The directors called all of us by name and managed to get everyone involved in programs, whether they were good or not. The softball teams included Midget Boys, Midget Girls, Junior Boys and Junior Girls. We held our practices on the playground with the leaders offering suggestions for improving our play to prepare us for games with other schools. Transportation was not provided for these inter-playground games so our rag-tag groups walked from one end of town to the other carrying balls, bats and the rest of our gear with us.

We didn't think anything of it because we were all used to walking; nevertheless we loved it when Anne Palmer invited us to pile in her snazzy, yellow convertible for the ride over. We sat three deep on the inside while others stood on the running board. We whooped, whistled and hollered all the

Dorothy Buss and Al Croft were our well-liked playground directors.

way, waving at everyone we saw. In spite of our raucous behavior, and whether we won or lost, Anne and leader Jane Gage usually treated us to an ice cream cone on the way back.

Other playground activities, arranged by the leaders, included volleyball, track meets and special games sometimes involving a big ball. The *Janesville Gazette* carried a weekly column on Playground Activity with news sent in by the playground directors. At one time or another during the summer, almost all of us had the thrill of seeing our name in print.

Stunt night, to which parents were invited, was a big occasion. Each of us had something to do; Solos, duets and group singing, skits, clowns, and dancing. My sister and I and four other girls learned the Highland Fling and also a jig to the tune of "An Irishman's Shanty". The music was scratched out by a small, wind-up Victrola.

Because of his strict upbringing, Papa did not approve of dancing but Mama didn't agree with him. Ruth and I swished, kicked and jigged in the house when he was not at home. When he was home, we practiced in the barn scaring our cow, Mollie, out of her wits. (Mama told us Mollie didn't give much milk on those nights.) Needless to say, we didn't invite Papa to Stunt Night where we performed vigorously, if not well.

With Stunt Night out of the way, we went back to sports. Early one afternoon in the midst of an exciting volleyball game, Dorothy Buss, the playground director that year, came over and said, "Finish up this game. I want you to come inside to make some necklaces."

"Do we have to?" I asked, not wanting to stop playing.

Dorothy's short blonde hair framed her pixy face as she tilted her head looking directly at me, her soft blue eyes on mine. She smiled, a sweet, almost angelic smile.

"Yes, Margie, it's part of the program," she said in her low-key manner.

I wanted to rebel. I thought of saying that I had to be home at a certain time—that I wasn't feeling well. But, I liked

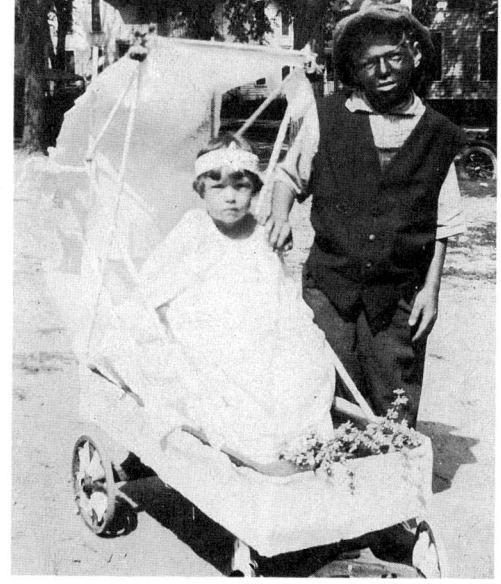

Ida's brother, Jake, pulls the Baby Queen, Dorothy Thom (Fenne), in the playground parade.

In the back row, tooting the horn for an upcoming playground production, is sister, Ruth. In the front row, are Beatrice Bissell and Ruth Thom as schoolgirls, Margaret Heath is dressed as a maid and Alice O'Gara as a farmer.

Dorothy. My feet dragged as I followed her inside.

In the basement, we sat at a long wood table. Dorothy handed out the supplies—tiny little beads of various colors, a long, thin needle and strong, waxed thread.

"We're going to learn to make Indian necklaces," she said, acting as though it was really something special.

Awkwardly, I picked up the needle. I had never held a needle before. Somehow, with encouragement, I managed to poke the thread through the eye and I started chasing the beads trying to pick them up with the needle and push them down the string.

Dorothy pointed out different color combinations and how to group several beads together to make a design.

"Isn't it time to go back out and play?" I asked.

"Not yet, Margie, we need to get more done on the necklaces," she said patiently. And again, that sweet, gentle smile.

I continued to sit there chasing little beads that kept getting away from me as I tried to poke the needle in them. At last, a few were beginning to stay in place. I made a design of different colored beads that looked like it could become a necklace. I couldn't believe it.

"You're doing fine, Margie," Dorothy said as she inquired if I needed any other colors, then added, "These necklaces make nice gifts." A gift, I thought to myself. Why would I want to make something and then give it away?

By the time I finished the first necklace, I began thinking it would be nice for Mama. It was really beautiful. Then I decided I would make another one so I would also have a Christmas gift for my favorite aunt, Aunt Mayme.

To get it done, I gave up precious outdoor time to work with the beads. It was a big sacrifice but I stuck with it and completed the necklaces in different colors and design. I was proud of my handiwork.

Although I planned to give them as Christmas gifts, I had to give Mama hers right away.

"This is lovely," exclaimed Mama. "Where did you get it?"

"I made it at the playground," I said puffing up.

Some of the members of the Midget softball team are shown here. Frankie Calumet is in the back row wearing a visor and my brother Rod is sitting in front.

"You made it? I don't believe it! I can't wait to show it to Papa," she said as she gave me a hug.

When Christmas finally came, I waited eagerly for Aunt Mayme to open her package.

"Margie, it's just beautiful, so artistic too. I shall treasure it forever knowing you made this for me all by yourself," Aunt Mayme said. It did look lovely on her dark, high-necked blouse. (For years to come, whenever we had a family function, she wore "my" necklace.)

I glowed with pride and satisfaction. She was not the easiest person in the world to please but I knew she liked it. As I was basking in the limelight, I felt good knowing I had forced myself to stay inside and work with the beads even when I didn't want to. I thought back about how it all came about.

"Our nice playground director, Dorothy Buss, talked me into doing it, and showed me how," I said, needing to express my appreciation too.

Members of the Senior softball team are shown here lined up by the school. In the back row, l - r, are Bub Kerl, Scottie Cochran, Howard (Gump) Anderson, Steve Hill and Ray Anderson.

I believe the boy on the left in the middle row is Ed Kerl and the handsome boy in the front row, wearing a beanie, looks like Jimmie Fitch. Douglas school produced some great baseball talent, especially Bub and Ed Kerl.

Chapter 17

The Power of Positive Thinking

Ruth, Rod, Marge, come on out to the rock! Ida called.

We hurried out, squeezing a place on the big platform in front of our house where other kids had already gathered.

"How many of you have warts?" Ida asked as soon as everyone was seated.

Several hands shot up including my brother Rod's and mine.

"Do you want to get rid of 'em?" she asked, looking intently from one to another.

"Yes, yes!" we yelled. My fingers, like many of the others, were dotted with warts which we were told was from handling toads and frogs.

"I know exactly what you can do to make them disappear," she said mysteriously.

"Tell us! Tell us how!" we said urging her to continue.

"Well, this is what you have to do. Wait until it gets dark, then tie a thread around each wart and go outside and bury a penny," she said in dead serious fashion.

Some of the kids scoffed and laughed but Ida simply ignored them and repeated the directions adding, "And there's one more thing. After you bury the penny, look at your fingers and imagine the warts are gone. That's the most important part. You've got to keep thinking the warts are gone!"

I believed Ida. So did my brother. We were sure it would work. That night we asked Mama for two pennies explaining why we needed them.

"I can't understand you kids. You believe everything Ida tells you," Mama replied, poking fun at our request.

Eventually, after much begging, she gave us the pennies. Rod and I helped one another tie the thread around our warts then headed outside to bury the pennies.

"No one is supposed to know where we bury them, so you go out in the back yard and I'll go by the side of the house," I said to Rod. Ida hadn't mentioned this but I thought it would be a good idea because if someone saw us and dug them up, I was afraid our warts wouldn't go away.

We each had a big tablespoon to dig with. As soon as I was sure no one was watching, I quickly dug a hole and buried my penny. Rod buried his and we met at the back porch.

"Now let's not forget, Ida said it was important to sit here, look at our hands and imagine all the warts are gone," Rod said.

We sat there for a few minutes concentrating on our fingers turning our hands around so we saw all of the bumps.

A little later, I started to shiver. "Let's go inside—it's getting sort of spooky out here tonight," I whispered to Rod.

Rod and I hurried into the house. We saw the look of amusement on Mama's face, and the big smirk on Ruth's. But, we still had faith.

A few days later, Ida called us together to inspect our hands. The scoffers still had their warts. Rod and I held our hands up high, "See, they're all gone!" we exclaimed. We were not at all surprised. We knew they would disappear.

"I told you so!" Ida said giving us a Mona Lisa smile.

She didn't say anything else. She probably didn't know about the powers of positive thinking. Or anything about "Your faith will make you well."

But Rod and I got the message.

Chapter 18

Spying on the Gypsies

"The Gypsies are coming," Ida shouted, pointing up Center Avenue hill.

Jake grabbed his knife ending our game of mumbletypeg as kids scattered in all directions. I took a quick look up the hill to make sure Ida wasn't just trying to scare us. One glimpse of the black touring car and I felt my skin crawl on the nape of my neck. I turned to run for home just one block away.

Usually I was a fast runner but today my bare feet didn't get any traction in the dirt. My legs felt rubbery like I was bouncing up and down in the same spot. My brother, Rod, and others ran past me as I struggled to get home. I knew what would happen to me if the Gypsies caught me. We had been warned, "The Gypsies steal kids. They take them away and they never see their family or friends again." My heart thumped like it was trying to get out of my body as I stumbled on. Through blurry eyes, I saw Mama waiting for me on the steps of the front porch. She quickly pulled me into the house and locked the door.

"Hide under the bed," she shouted, pulling down all the downstairs window shades. We knew Mama was just as scared as we were.

"I hear them coming. I'm going to peek out," Mama said as she pulled back the frayed, green window shade a fraction of an inch.

"There's a long black touring car. It has the side enclosures on so I can't see inside," she whispered. "Here comes another car just like it. And another. There's four cars in the caravan, all with side enclosures." Rod and I listened from under the bed as she continued, " Oh Good! There's two policemen on motorcycles right behind them to escort them out of town. They'll make sure they don't stop!" Mama sounded relieved.

When we heard the police were there, Rod and I had enough courage to crawl out from under the bed and take a quick look. "I wish I could see them better, I can't tell what they really look like," I complained before sliding back under the bed. With the presence of the police, the tension lessened. Nevertheless, it was almost an hour before Mama raised the shades and unlocked the doors.

Why were we so terrified of Gypsies? Living on the outskirts of town, we crossed paths with tramps and hoboes almost every day. One at a time, they came to our door regularly to beg for something to eat. (Papa said they had our house marked.) Mama always fixed a big plate of food for them which they ate on the back porch. Why was it we were not the least bit afraid of tramps and hoboes, yet, the Gypsies scared us out of our wits?

It had to be the stories we heard. "Two Gypsy women kidnapped a seven-year old boy from a farm in Green County while the men talked to the farmer. He was never seen again." Or, "They wrangled their way into the home of an elderly couple and stole their life savings from under the mattress on their bed right while the wife was resting on it." A neighbor had another episode to tell, "I saw this Gypsy woman sneak in my chicken coop and come out with a big bulge under her skirt but I was too scared to yell at her or try to stop her. You never know what they might do."

Papa's favorite story was about the time they short-changed the clerk at Roesling's grocery. The next year when they came, the owner, Mr. Roesling, said, "I'm going to stand right at the register and watch every transaction. They're not getting away with anything this time." In spite of his careful supervision, when they settled up the day's sales, they found the till was $40.00 short. Everyone said, "They're clever and they're quick."

The unlawful behaviour of the Gypsies was related over and over again whenever they came to town. But our friend, Ida, had another version.

"They are beautiful people, very artistic and musical," she told us.

"Why do they steal everything?" we asked.

"Because they have to eat as they go from place to place," she explained.

"Why don't they settle down and get jobs?" my sister, the practical one, asked.

"Well, that's not their way," Ida said in an indignant, defensive tone, "they're romantic roamers who don't want to stay in one place. They never have."

"Couldn't they change so they won't end up in jail?" my sister persisted.

"It's not easy to change the way you live. Most people just go on and on, stuck with the life they're used to," Ida replied in her worldly fashion.

"Do you want to go with me tonight to watch them sing and dance around the campfire? They're camping on Western Avenue, just up the hill past Courtney's. Do you want to go?" Ida asked.

We all shrunk back.

"The women are really pretty with dark wavy hair and black eyes. They wear bright, beautiful clothes and lots of jewelry," she went on.

"How do you know?" My sister asked. We had never really seen a Gypsy up close—only a quick glimpse from behind a curtain when they came by in horse-drawn wagons and later in cars.

"I've watched them and they're real nice. They're not bad like everyone says," Ida replied. "We can watch from the ditch by the road and they'll never know we're there. Do you want to go see their camp or not?" Ida looked around to see if there were any takers.

"What if they catch us?" I asked in a trembling voice.

"They're not gonna catch us—and besides what would they want with us? Just more mouths to feed," she said.

We weren't interested in her suggestion. We were too scared. But, she had raised our curiosity—so much so, that by the time the sun went down, my brother and I had decided to go, assuring ourselves that "Ruth will stay home and if we don't come back, she'll tell Papa and he will come to get us."

With Ida in the lead, we set out at dusk to spy on the Gypsies, knowing full well we shouldn't be going, yet eager to watch them dance and listen to their music.

"Hurry up, do you want to go or not?" Ida asked as Rod and I dragged our feet along the dark, dusty road.

I could hear Mama's exasperated voice ringing in my ears, "That girl can get you to do anything." I knew it was true. I was trapped in the web of excitement woven by Ida's mystical power. As we neared the encampment, I wondered what I was doing there. I wanted to turn around and run for home. But I didn't. The web was too strong.

A few minutes later, Ida put her finger to her mouth and pointed to the stake out spot. "Lie down in the ditch and don't make a sound 'til I look around," Ida whispered. Rod and I buried ouselves in the tall weeds. From the way the weeds were swaying, I realized I wasn't the only spy who was trembling.

Ida found a vantage point on the high side of the ditch behind a big bush. "They're building a fire. One of them is carrying water." She described the action in a hushed, scary voice. "Now they're taking some chickens out of a gunny sack. I'll bet they stole 'em. Come on up and take a look, but be quiet!"

Warily, Rod and I crept up the bank. We saw feathers flying as two women plucked the chickens. We smelled the smoke as the fire started to blaze. A child was crying, another one whining. We heard angry, harsh voices.

"Why aren't they singing and dancing?" I whispered.

"Because they're doing their chores," she replied.

"They aren't wearing pretty clothes. They look tired," Rod

said, disappointed.

"They're dusty and dirty and have work to do," Ida explained.

Just then one of the Gypsy men stood up and glanced in our direction.

"They heard us. They know we're here and they're coming after us," Ida uttered under her breath. We bolted out of there.

Down the road we flew at breakneck speed. We didn't look back to see if we were being followed. Rod and I burst into the kitchen, out of breath, startling Mama, Papa, and Ruth sitting at the kitchen table.

"Why don't you share with us what Ida just told you? It must be really good," Mama said. Ruth just smiled.

Rod and I didn't say anything. I went right upstairs. I was tempted to hide under the bed but I didn't. I shook as I crawled under the covers. But besides being scared, I felt sad. Sad because the Gypsies weren't happy and carefree, sad that they weren't singing and dancing and sad because they were tired and cross. And, most of all, I was sad because they couldn't change their ways. They, too, were caught in a web.

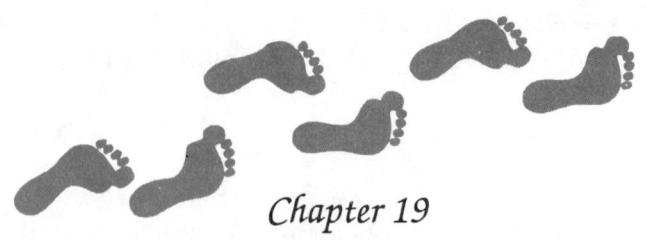

Chapter 19

Summer Vacations

"The mice are getting out of hand so bring some kittens when you come," Aunt Lizzie had written to Mama before we left to spend our summer vacation with Mama's sister, her husband Ollie and family at their cheese factory south of Juda, WI. Although Mama and us kids spent our one week summer vacation visiting Mama's sisters and brothers in Green County, Papa always worked and never got time off to go with us.

When it was time to leave for the train depot, Mama carefully placed six little striped kittens in a box lined with paper and rags and put the box in the bottom of a gunny sack.

"I'll carry them," Rod said, as we were packed and ready to leave.

"Try to hold them still," Mama cautioned as she saw Rod swinging the bag as we walked up Center Avenue hill on the way to the depot.

We were early and could hardly wait until the train came. We heard a shrill whistle in the distance, then bells ringing as the crossing gates went down. We stood on the edge of the platform as the train choo-choo-chooed toward us, slowed down and stopped. The hissing and clouds of steam from the engine sent us close to Mama as we heard the rhythmic clash of metal as one railroad car bumped into the one in front of it. This was not our first train ride, but it was always scary to be that close to the huge, noisy locomotive belching and hissing.

The door of the coach opened. The conductor placed a

step-stool on the platform and helped the arriving passengers as they climbed down the steps carrying their suitcases. It was now time for us to climb on board. Mama and Ruth each carried a suitcase, Rod had the gunny sack filled with kittens and I had a bag of cookies to eat on the way.

The conductor helped Mama put the suitcases in the rack over our heads but Rod held tightly to the gunnysack which he put by his feet. We waited and watched while the luggage, baggage and mail were taken off the train, and then while more big wagons were wheeled out with more luggage, baggage and mail to be loaded. After what seemed like a long time, we watched the conductor go back down the railroad car steps. Holding on to the railing with one hand, he leaned out, extending as far as possible, then waved his hand in a big semi circle, booming out, "All Aboard!"

With a sudden lurch, we were on our way. The time passed quickly as Rod, Ruth and I made frequent trips up and down the swaying coach to get drinks of water in small paper cups to wash down the cookies. We tried out the toilets and could see the tracks sailing by below.

"That's why the sign says you can't use the toilets while the train is stopped at the station—all that stuff would smell up the place," Ruth told me.

It wasn't long before the conductor came in. "Brodhead, next stop. Brodhead," he called out as he went through the car.

"Be careful with the kittens, Rodney," Mama said as the train slowed down and we were gathering our things.

Uncle Ollie was waiting for us up at the depot. Ollie was born in Switzerland and didn't speak much English. He was dark complected with dark, bushy hair and a big mustache. When he saw us, his face broke into a big grin.

"I buy new car, yah," he said as he helped Mama with the luggage. "First time I drive," he added, nodding his head up and down vigorously, still grinning proudly.

He cranked the car and after a jerky start, we headed off for his cheese factory west of Brodhead. The car stopped a couple times but he was cheerful and patient as he got out, cranked it and got it started again. Everything seemed to be going all right but we held our breath as he drove through the covered bridge over the Sugar River—the Clarence Bridge. When we arrived at the cheese factory, we saw Aunt Lizzie out in the yard waving to us. Uncle Ollie turned into the driveway and headed for a small shed where he kept the car. The car didn't slow down.

"Whoa, whoa," he yelled as he pulled back on the steering wheel. "Whoa, Whoa," he shouted, pulling harder on the wheel. As we got closer to the shed with the car continuing to speed along, Uncle Ollie stood up as he tugged at the wheel shouting "WHOA!" In spite of Ollie's shouting and tugging, the car kept going. The front of the shed was open as the car entered. On we went. A few seconds later we crashed into the wall at the back of the shed. The boards splintered making a terrible racket and the car shuddered to a stop.

Us kids were scared out of our wits and sat frozen in our seats. The kittens were yowling so Rod grabbed the gunny sack and held them on his lap. Then Mama started to laugh.

"Ollie, you forgot you were driving a car - not a team of horses," she gasped as she laughed some more, wiping tears from her eyes. Ollie wasn't laughing. His face was red as he helped us unpack and carry our stuff to their living quarters over the cheese factory.

"We brought you some pretty kittens," Rod said, as soon as we got settled and Mama had stopped laughing. He untied the string and opened the sack. The kittens jumped out and scattered in all directions. Suddenly kittens were everywhere, flying up and down the chairs and over the sofa, up the lace curtains across the top and then back down.

"They must be having a fit," Mama said. "Try to catch them and calm them down."

Then it was Aunt Lizzie who started to laugh. She doubled over, howling in glee as she watched Mama and us kids frantically chasing the fast-moving kittens. We found out they were hard to catch. Our friendly little kittens had become wild tigers, hissing and scratching. A couple of the kittens caught

Cousins Betty and Bob Huggler are shown here with the kittens who almost tore up their house.

their claws in the lace curtains, making holes in them. When we tried to pry them loose from the curtains, their claws shredded the lace. It felt like they were doing the same to our arms and hands. We cornered some of the kittens then snatched them by the back of their neck holding them away from us as they hissed and clawed struggling to get free when we dumped them back in the gunny sack. All the time Aunt Lizzie shrieked with laughter.

"It's not funny, Lizzie. Look what they're doing to your lace curtains," Mama said as she managed to get the last kitten under control.

"I need new ones anyway," Aunt Lizzie gasped in between peels of laughter. She continued to laugh as we got the kittens settled down. Then I remembered that everything was funny to her. She laughed even when I stubbed my toe while running and skidded all the way across the floor on my belly. I never understood why she found that so hilarious either.

Nevertheless, we all liked Aunt Lizzie. She came to visit us often with Pembroke, her son by a previous marriage. She played with us and was always a lot of fun. When we visited her, she went out of her way to make sure we had a good time. One time when Rod shot a pigeon in their barn, she dressed it and cooked it for him. She fixed us delicious desserts using rich cream from the milk neighboring farmers hauled in big metal containers, on horse-drawn wagons or Model T Fords, to Uncle Ollie's cheese factory. The milk was dumped in huge, glistening copper vats and ended up as brick cheese.

Aunt Lizzie had a Victrola with a diamond needle which we kept winding up and playing. We sang and danced as we listened to Caruso, Henry Lauder singing "Roamin' in the Gloamin" and then our favorite, "How Much is that Doggie in the Window?".

On another vacation, when we planned to visit Aunt Rosa and Uncle Dave in New Glarus, Mama said, "Now don't tell Ida we're going, or her mother will send her along with us."

In previous years, Ida's mother would send her on the train with us so Ida could visit her relatives there much to Mama's annoyance.

"I put up with that girl all year and I'm not putting up with her on my vacation," Mama told us, again warning us not to tell Ida where we were going.

In preparation for the vacation, Mama made navy blue serge skirts and capes, lined with red satin, for Ruth and me and a navy blue suit for Rod. She was anxious that we look good.

The day of the big trip arrived and Ida still didn't know about it. Mama was more than relieved, she was elated. But, not for long.

Less than an hour before we were to leave, Ida's mother came running across the street. In her excitement and haste, she spoke partly Swiss and English, "I get Eda ready, you take, yah?"

Mama was fit to be tied but she couldn't refuse.

As we were leaving for the train depot, Mama looked us over, proud of how we looked in our new finery—then at Ida in her big black bloomers, carrying a paper sack with her belongings.

Of course us kids were delighted to have Ida along, especially Ruth, who might have leaked the news of our trip. (Although it could have been Papa. He didn't like it when Mama acted "uppity" as he put it.) Ruth and Ida were sitting two rows ahead of Mama, Rod and I on the train, laughing and talking. Mama was a little glum.

One of Ida's traits that Mama was not familiar with, but would soon learn about, was Ida's ability to pass gas. She was completely natural about it and had the earthy way of raising one buttock to let it escape. Afterwards, she seemed relieved and pleased with herself; the louder the better, never the least bit embarrassed.

"It's because she's from Europe," Ruth told Rod and me one night when we were discussing this habit, which we had been taught was pretty disgusting.

As we were riding along, the coach was quiet when suddenly, the quietness was broken with a loud, drawn out poop, much like a balloon slowly bursting. The noise was accompanied by a putrid smell. All heads turned towards Ida and Ruth.

"Why, Ruth," Ida said loud and clear, as she turned toward her raising her eyebrows in an expression of total disgust.

Mama gasped. Even though she didn't know about this trait, she knew who the culprit was. Her face turned every possible shade of red to livid purple. She took off the jacket of her new gold suit. She squirmed. With a jerky movement, she pulled out the hat pin and removed her hat, using it to fan herself.

When Mama was finally able to speak, all she could mutter was "That girl . . . that girl!"

Aunt Rosa and Uncle Dave, who had no children, lived in a big white house in New Glarus. It was on a hill a few blocks from downtown. They had a big barn and an attached chicken coop where they raised chickens. We watched the big incubator that kept the eggs warm so they would hatch. We were fascinated when an egg started to crack and a little chick worked its way out.

And we loved seeing and playing with the fluffy yellow chicks.

On the streets downtown, and in the stores, the people spoke Swiss. Everyone greeted us and spoke to us. We smiled and nodded even though we couldn't understand them.

Uncle Dave owned several farms and was considered well off but would only spend money for the bare necessities. Aunt Rosie spent her spare time making quilts. When she sold them, she gave the money to her husband. Aunt Rosa scrimped all year, hiding a penny away at a time, so she could treat us to a five cent ice cream cone when we came to visit. Then we had to sneak around so Dave wouldn't see us enter the bakery/ice cream store.

Every meal consisted of a boiled ring of bologna and potatoes boiled with the jackets on. A variation was having fried potatoes. With each meal was Aunt Rosa's home made bread and strawberry jam which we enjoyed, along with her ginger cookies.

We never stayed more than a couple days in New Glarus so we could spend most of our time at Uncle Chris's farm west of Monroe. Chris was an older brother who was born in Switzerland. He was powerfully built with dark skin, black hair and an outstanding, well-cared for, handlebar mustache.

His wife was Elizabeth but was nicknamed "Lizzie". We always called her 'Aunt Lizzie Chris' to differentiate her from the many Lizzie's in the family. They had two children, Helen and Lee, who were young adults living and working at home. They also took care of my cousin, Stanley, whose mother died at our house with the flu. Also in the household were two hired men who lived with the family.

I learned the role of a farmer's wife from watching Aunt Lizzie Chris. She got up at four o'clock, lit the kerosene lamps and got ready for her busy schedule. First she went out to the barn to milk 'her' cows, usually eight or nine, while Chris and the hired help milked the others. Then she bustled up the grade to the house to prepare breakfast on the cook stove. When she had the fire going, she fried thick slices of bacon, eggs and crispy potatoes. This she served with home made bread, grape jelly, cake and strong coffee.

Aunt Lizzie Chris was a short woman. She looked like a little girl dressed up in her mother's long dress, apron and small white cap. Her cheeks were rosy and her blue eyes sparkled as she continued her chores taking feed to the chickens. "Here chick, chick," she called. The chicks cluck-clucked as they came running to her. She held the bucket low and scattered the feed evenly amongst her brood. She looked them over carefully to make sure they were all right.

Seeing how busy she was, Rod and I offered to help her. "Why don't you go to the hen house and gather the eggs?" she suggested.

She gave us some buckets and we skipped happily on our way. We quickly retrieved the eggs in the empty nests, then it was time to face the haughty, matronly hens who did not want to give up their eggs. As I reached timidly toward the nest, the hen looked me right in the eye and pecked at me. That was enough to convince me she was ready to poke out my eyes if I dared to reach in the nest. Rod was having the same experience. It wasn't the chickens that chickened out that day.

When we took the eggs in the house, Aunt Lizzie Chris noticed there weren't the usual number of eggs but didn't say anything to embarrass us. She understood we tried. Then my cousin Stanley, who was my age, noticed something else in the basket.

"Hah, look! They don't know the difference between a glass egg and a real egg," he guffawed, "city kids are sure dumb".

"We put those glass eggs in the nests to encourage the hens to lay," our aunt explained to us while Stanley and one of the hired men kept on teasing us. Rod's ears were bright red and he ran outside and tried to hide. I followed him.

"They don't like us. They don't want us here," he said.

"They're just having fun," I tried to explain.

"You think everyone likes us but they don't," he replied.

I made him come back in the house where Aunt Lizzie Chris greeted us with a sugar cookie telling us she was grateful for our help. "We're having chicken for supper," she told us.

We watched this gentle little woman grab a twenty-two rifle and walk outside. She had already decided which ones she would do in. She picked them out from the others and shot them right in the eye, rushed over and snapped their necks. She then grabbed a sharp cleaver and with one chop severed their heads. We watched in horror as the heads flew off, blood gushed out and the headless chickens danced aimlessly around the yard.

In that awful moment, I learned the meaning of the expression, "Running around like a chicken with his head cut off."

Nauseated as we were by this terrible sight, Rod and I somehow had regained our appetites by the time the big platters of fried chicken reached the dinner table.

As soon as the meal was over and the men went in the living room, dishes were picked up and washed immediately with hot water dipped from the stove reservoir into a big dish pan. Everything was done when it should be done, quickly and efficiently, to make time for tending the garden, canning the vegetables, fruit and meat. (The tastiest, most tender meat I've ever eaten.)

In a shed outside the farmhouse was where Aunt Lizzie Chris did the laundry. She scrubbed the clothes on the washboard, using Fels Naphtha soap when she ran out of her home-made soap. She rinsed them, wringing the bulky articles with snaps and buckles by hand. The others she fed through the wringer with one hand while turning the handle with the other. Then she hung them out on the line to dry. She stretched to hang the heavy bib overalls on the line, dwarfed by their size.

The next day she faced several baskets of ironing. She heated the irons on the stove, then guided the heavy iron with quick, efficient movements, putting aside any articles that needed mending.

She was a good manager but Uncle Chris didn't appreciate her comments when he sat with his hired help at the table to discuss what should be planted in what field, and when and how the work should be done. She sat away from the table, her head bent over a sock she was mending, but close enough so she could listen carefully to the discussion. She only offered a suggestion when she felt it was necessary, usually in the form of a question, "Chris, I wonder if you think it might be better to plow the back forty first?" She would then explain the reasons in a meek, quiet manner. Sometimes this approach worked, but usually thin-skinned, hot-headed Chris would shout, "Shut up, woman!"

I liked Uncle Chris a lot, but couldn't understand how Aunt Lizzie Chris could handle these rebuffs. Mama explained, "They love each other and she understands him, that's why she always puts his feelings above hers". I wasn't sure I could do that.

Uncle Chris was an outgoing person who enjoyed being surrounded by a lot of company—which added to Aunt Lizzie Chris's work as she served them wine and food. But she joined in the singing and yodeling, and never complained.

One time when we were visiting, my cousin Lee rented a radio. We sat in the living room, huddled around it, trying to be close enough to it to hear Rudy Vallee sing above the static. Suddenly the big horn on top of the radio lurched forward.

"What the Hell!" Lee shouted as he grabbed it to keep it from falling. He saw the wires were jiggling and pulling the horn toward the window so he disconnected the wires, and looked out the window.

"The horses got out and they're eating the bushes by the window," he shouted. They were also eating the wires, pulling the radio toward the window.

"Come out and help get the horses in!" Uncle Chris shouted as he cussed the horses. Lee cussed and yelled. And Stanley, not to be outdone, added his curses to the melee. I was scared because of the cussing and commotion. I was also scared of the horses but I made myself stand where they told me to and wave my arms when the horses came near. When the horses were back in the pasture, Lee re-connected the radio so we could listen some more.

One of the most exciting times at Uncle Chris's was when they had threshers. Aunt Lizzie Chris and Helen baked for days to prepare for it. I carried water to the fields for the men and helped serve the incredible amount and variety of food. I couldn't believe the way the workers put away the food as I kept refilling the dishes.

Summer vacations end and we go home knowing more about our relatives and how their lives differ from ours.

An important part of our farm vacations was playing with the pets.

Chapter 20

Holidays

The holidays we celebrated were Easter, a holy day; Decoration Day, when we remembered the dead; the Fourth of July, a patriotic occasion; Thanksgiving, when the focus was on our early history, and Christmas, which was partly religious, but mostly a fun time.

Weeks before Easter, Mama started sewing dresses with layers of organdy for Ruth and me to wear to church and parties. We sometimes also got new slippers. Another of Mama's tasks was to color hard boiled eggs for us. She covered them with moist leaves, then wrapped a cloth around them letting them stand overnight. On Easter morning, she didn't hide them but placed them in a bowl on the dining room table. As we sat down for breakfast, she gave each of us a brown and tan egg with a delicate leaf pattern on it. She also gave us a penny sack of candy - which was more important to us than the eggs which Mama worked on for hours.

Getting ready for church on Easter Sunday was not easy. We never seemed to look as good as Mama wanted us to look. She kept re-tying my sash and straightening my stockings. If it was cold out, I had to wear long underwear which was hard to smooth out so it wouldn't show ridges. Then we usually got a late start and had to run most of the way. Although the church was filled with woman wearing their new Easter bonnets, men in suit and tie and kids all gussied up, our parents did not attend—along with many other parents who regularly sent their kids to Sunday School but who did not attend the

In the Monterey neighborhood, church was an important part of life. Here, Rod, Ruth and I (clutching the Bible) are on our way to church.

church services.

One Easter, the Sunday School Superintendent gave out pins to students who hadn't missed a Sunday. He had a remark or two for each recipient.

"Beatrice, you have shown how much you enjoy Sunday School by your perfect attendance," he beamed as he presented the pin to one of the older girls.

"Thank you. I'm getting a pin because my folks send me every Sunday" she said as she accepted the pin, "they like to be alone so they can go back to bed." A few gasps could be heard throughout the church.

On Decoration Day, we walked to Oak Hill Cemetery with armsful of lilacs, iris, and whatever else might be in bloom.

On Decoration Day, Aunt Mayme (l) and Mama take flowers to the cemetery.

First we went to where my brother was buried at the foot of Papa's grandmother's grave. Mama said, "How I wish we could have a marker for little Donald," as the tears rolled down her cheeks. From the cemetery we walked downtown to see the parade. Mama and Papa clapped and cheered loudly whenever the flag passed by. You could tell they really loved their country and appreciated the important role of the war veterans.

On the Fourth of July, Mama fixed a picnic lunch and we took the train to Brodhead to meet Mama's family for the big celebration in the park next to the train depot. Papa didn't come with us, but before we left he gave us some 'snakes', small, grey, pill-like objects that, when lit, would expand sending a long band of ash like material curling and slithering out, resembling a snake. It also sent forth a putrid sulfur smell. We rode on carnival rides and stuffed ourselves with ice cream and goodies with nickels provided by our uncles. All the aunts, uncles and cousins gathered together, sitting on blankets, as we shared the picnic lunches. After we watched the water fights and tug-o-wars, it was then time to say goodby's and catch the train home.

On Thanksgiving, Papa's sisters and families came to our house. Uncle Perce MaGee and Aunt Mayme drove their graceful cutter pulled by a team of horses from their farm five miles out on the Evansville Road. They stopped enroute to pick up Aunt Ella and Uncle Ben Parish, who lived by the Four-Mile Bridge. In later years, he drove his new touring car with side enclosures to keep out the cold. Sometimes Aunt Elizabeth and Uncle Ed Butterfield came from Michigan with their son, Lee, who was a few years older than us. It was always more fun when they came.

Mama baked and fussed all week to prepare the turkey and all the trimmings. After everyone arrived, Rod, Ruth and I donned our pilgrim costumes to perform a skit we did at school. Then Papa said the Thanksgiving prayer and we sat down to eat. Mama was nervous as she served the food. She was never comfortable around Papa's family and more so today as she was afraid the dinner wouldn't come up to their expectations. Of course it did, and she finally relaxed after they all complimented her on the turkey, dressing, cranberries, mashed potatoes, squash and pumpkin pie.

Christmas was special, not because of the gifts because we didn't get many, but for the feelings of joy and expectation. We enjoyed preparing for our school program and could hardly wait for the big day to come followed by a two week vacation. We were also in a program at church, an evening pageant depicting the birth of Jesus. Each child had a part and at the conclusion we sang Christmas carols until Santa arrived with a candy cane for each child.

Our family Christmas was always spent at Aunt Mayme's. Aunt Mayme was always very special to me. Her long, reddish hair was combed up and corralled in a loose bun arrangement on top of her head. Her deep-set, blue eyes were crowned with expressive eyebrows which she used to show surprise, anger, and disgust, as well as approval. She was tall, thin and poised, always in control. She was the person I admired the most. I knew she liked me too, although she never told me she did. She never displayed affection by hugging or kissing.

Aunt Mayme's farm home was genteel and interesting, from the carpeted floors and lace curtains to the profusion of Boston ferns spreading out from their basket containers almost concealing the tall, narrow tables. The dining room's focal point was an oak buffet with a mirror reflecting an elegant china tea service and a white, hand-painted hot chocolate set.

The den was always dark. A small round table held a kerosene lamp, the family Bible and special glasses that Uncle Perce called steriopticans. We took turns looking through them to see photographs in 3-dimension, spectacular pictures of mountains, lakes and scenery that looked so real you wanted to reach out and touch them. It also had a black leather couch on the far end where Uncle Perce took his afternoon nap. A bookcase with glass doors and a secretary/desk was just inside the door. This is where Uncle Perce wrote in his journal every day—always including a description of the weather, farm news and how the Cubs were doing. Pictures in the den included "The Reaper" and "The Thresher". Aunt Mayme unlocked the glassed-in bookcase so we could look at the special books and the National Geographic magazines.

The front room was light and spacious. Unlike most families, they used their living room, not reserving it only for company. Uncle Perce kept his radio there with his chair directly in front of it. During the baseball season, he practically stuck his head in the box in order to hear the announcer over the loud static. The Cubs were his pride and joy, even when they lost.

The most wondrous part of the home was a small room,

probably used as a pantry at one time, just off the den. This little area was Aunt Mayme's treasure cove where she kept correspondence, books, games, bean bags she had made, a croquet set and the many gifts sent to her by her only child, a son, George Lyman MaGee, who lived in the Philippine Islands. We didn't go in the little room, but sat on the floor outside as Aunt Mayme went in and brought out special items to show us. Perhaps an envelope with many beautiful stamps on it and a letter in George's fine handwriting. She read it aloud to us providing us with a glimpse of what life was like in that far away world. Then she brought out some of the articles he had sent, beautiful baskets in various shapes and colors. She explained how the natives made them. She held up an exquisite lace tablecloth. Just the way she touched it and handled it, we knew it was precious. She told us how the lace was made. She showed us woven skirts, scarves, and "G-Strings" which the natives wore.

Then came little objects such as elephants hand carved from ivory or ebony with ivory tusks. We were pretty sure we would be getting one of these as Christmas gifts and we couldn't wait for dinner to be served so we could open our gift.

But before that, after the table had been cleared and the dishes washed, Aunt Mayme sat down in her small rocker with the three of us at her feet to read, Charles Dicken's A CHRISTMAS CAROL. We sat spell-bound as she read, sometimes wiping away tears when she read of Tiny Tim. I don't know how long it took but we never moved—we were carried away by her words. (Many years later, my brother, Rod, decided to carry on this tradition when his son was young. He summoned his son along with nieces and nephews and started to read this great story which we had enjoyed so much. They squirmed, complained, wiggled and giggled and paid no attention to the story. Rod yelled at them to listen. He shouted "shut up, and be quiet"—but it didn't work. In disgust, he had to give up. Another tradition bit the dust.)

In the summertime we had picnics at Aunt Mayme's. We

A friendly cow is licking my sister's face during a picnic at Aunt Mayme's.

walked down the lane to the pasture where there was a water area created by artesian springs. Here we walked on the rocks and picked watercress. We also picked hazel nuts and gooseberries. Aunt Mayme spread a blanket down and opened the basket containing the food. As we sat there eating, it was not unusual to have a cow, or two, come along and lick our faces.

Staying at Aunt Mayme's overnight was also a special treat but not until we got over our fear of the blackness of the night in rural areas. In the city, there was always a street light, in the country it was a vast, big black emptiness.

While staying at Aunt Mayme's, we liked her custom of serving tea at 4 o'clock, sometimes in the living room and other times on the side porch. She placed a bouquet of fresh flowers on the table, put on her lace tea apron, and poured us hot chocolate from a beautiful, graceful pitcher she kept on the buffet. She served us big, round sugar cookies from a plate which she had hand-painted. This ritual called for our best behaviour.

I liked visiting Aunt Mayme. I hoped someday I could have a home like hers in the country alongside a lake or river. And, in spite of what others said about her being bossy, (she only told people what they should know but didn't want to hear) I wanted to be just like her.

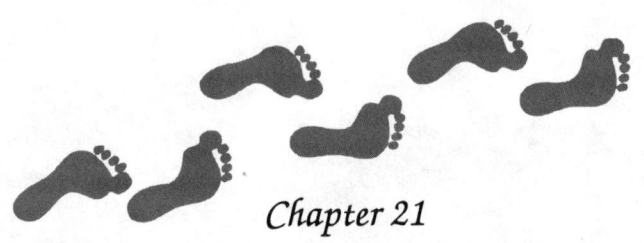

Chapter 21

Snow Time

"Have you looked out the window?" Mama asked with a big grin as Rod, Ruth and I came trooping down the steps for breakfast on the Saturday after Christmas.

"WOW!" Rod screamed as he saw the ground blanketed with snow, "now we can try out our new Flexible Flyer." We were ready when we heard Ida's call.

"Ruth, Rod, Marge, come on out. We're going sliding!" Ida was at the back porch with her brother, Jake, who was pulling the stubby sled his father made for him for Christmas. Although it was made from scraps of lumber, two coats of red paint gave it a sparkling look. Rod quickly maneuvered our sled from the back porch and we hurried across the road to Bumper Hill which ran parallel to the railroad bank on the left with huge oil storage tanks on the right.

Under a cloudless, deep blue sky, the fresh snow shimmered on the steep incline already dotted with screaming, laughing kids. As we climbed the hill, friends came sailing past, sometimes three or four deep, as one rider belly-flopped atop another. Sometimes they became top heavy and lost their balance, then, one after another rolled off on to the soft snow. We lent a hand to pull up the snow-imbedded bodies sprawled on the hillside. Some kids, who didn't have sleds, skidded by on large pieces of cardboard, others on metal trays.

Although there were other places to slide, we liked Bumper Hill the best. It was just steep enough and it had several bumps along the way that jolted us up in the air. We didn't worry about sliding out on Western Avenue as there was very little traffic.

"Margie, your cheeks are as red as your new scarf," Ida said, as we neared the top. I knew it was true because I felt my cheeks burning with excitement.

"For the first trip down, the three of us will go together," Ruth announced, "then we'll take turns going alone."

Rod, Ruth and I positioned ourselves on the new Flexible Flyer, all sitting up. Ida gave us a push as we started down with Rod steering the bars with his feet. The wind brushed our faces, and my heart pounded as we sped at breakneck speed down the bumpy hill.

"It's as fast as Papa said it would be," Ruth exclaimed.

"Isn't this fun?" I asked Jake as we pulled the sled back up the hill.

"Not for me," he said, "my sled isn't working. When I run and jump on it, the runners sink in the snow." He explained that he tried sitting up, pushing himself along, but was annoyed when the other kids raced by on their faster sleds. "I wish I had a sled like yours so I could go fast."

While we were talking Ruth and Rod took their turns and it was my time to go down alone. I picked up the sled, ran a few steps then belly-flopped on the sled. I had only gone a short ways when Jake belly-flopped on top of me. I gasped as the air squished out of me. Roughly, he put his hands over mine on the steering bar.

"Hey, this is great," Jake called out as we picked up speed, his face close to mine.

When we neared the bottom of the hill, Jake dragged his right foot, pushed the steering bar hard to the right. The abrupt turn sent both of us sprawling in the fresh bed of snow.

Jake jumped up. He watched as I slowly sat up.

"Are you all right? I didn't hurt you, did I?" Jake asked as he leaned over me.

I looked up at him, surprised at the worried look in his grey eyes. I wasn't hurt but I couldn't say anything.

"I wouldn't hurt you for anything in the world, Margie. I

like you," Jake blurted out.

"I'm all right, Jake. You didn't hurt me," I said as I felt the tears coming.

"Are you sure?" he asked, seeing the tears.

"Honest, I'm fine." I dabbed away at the tears with my red scarf, wondering why the tears kept coming when I was feeling so warm and wonderful.

Back on top of the hill, Ruth and Rod saw what happened and came sliding, slipping and skidding down.

Ruth glared at Jake, wagging her forefinger in his face. "I suppose you think you're big stuff rolling the sled over," she screamed. "Next time pick on somebody your own size, you big roughneck."

Jake opened his mouth to yell back at Ruth, but he stopped. I guess he'd never yelled at a girl before except his sister, Ida.

"I didn't mean to hurt her. Why do I always get in trouble with girls? I didn't mean to do anything wrong," he said.

"Just go play with your rough friends, you big bully!" Ruth shouted waving her arm for him to leave.

"Ruth, don't blame Jake. He didn't hurt me. I think I was just scared," I said, unable to understand my feelings.

"I'll pull the sled up," Jake volunteered as he smiled at me. Ruth calmed down and we all started up the hill together. Part way up the hill, we jumped to one side as some of the older boys came speeding past on a sheet of corrugated tin, rolled up at the front edge to resemble a toboggan. They usually slid on the steep Miltimore Hill across the river so we were surprised to see them here.

"It's the fastest thing on the hill. Even faster than our Flexible Flyer—it really streaks," Rod told Papa as we sat around the dining room table talking about how much fun we had sledding that day. Rod went on to explain that the big boys made it out of a sheet of corrugated tin and curled up the front edge.

"It sounds dangerous to me," Papa responded, not very impressed, "If they hit something at that speed, they could get cut up really bad."

It seemed to me that Papa was always seeing the danger in everything. I was glad Rod didn't tell Papa that the boys who designed it sometimes added water to the hill to make it go even faster.

"Don't you kids ever get on that thing," Papa cautioned. Apparently Ruth wasn't listening because the very next day she happily went on a ride in space as ballast on the tin toboggan.

It started out with the big boys asking us to help them build a snow ramp on the railroad bank between our house and Hagar's. We were always glad when they noticed us and were anxious to help. We got buckets and started hauling snow from the nearby areas. The railroad bank from the ground up was steep, then there was a wide flat area, the plateau where we had our path and Mulligan stews, then another steep incline up to the railroad tracks.

Later on when we were getting tired and slowing down, the older kids explained the plan. "We'll take the tin toboggan to the top of the bank on the railroad tracks, slide down the steep short hill where we'll pick up a lot of speed, then we'll level off in the flat area here, and hit the ramp. We should take off like an airplane."

It sounded pretty exciting to me - yet dangerous. I guess I was worried about what Papa said. But, knowing the plan, we kept on hauling snow which the bigger boys packed down to form a ramp resembling a ski jump.

To me, the big boys seemed like super engineers. I had watched them handle the sleek, grey metal thingamajig on the steep, treacherous Miltimore hill across the river. They glided at top speed, coasted and turned to miss the trees. I was sure they knew what they were doing.

Late in the afternoon, the big kids inspected the ramp and were satisfied that it was ready. They huddled together to make the final plans. "Two of us will go on the maiden voyage," the biggest one said. Then he picked out another boy to go with him. As they were ready to go up the bank to the tracks, the leader said, "We need a small kid for ballast."

He pointed to my sister.

"No! No!," Rod yelled. But Ruth quickly followed them up the hill, while Rod raced for home to tell Mama and Papa.

The two big boys and the 'ballast' settled down on the tin sheet. .When all was ready, helpers pushed them off to give them a good start. They slid down the steep embankment at a fast clip, flattening out as they reached the plateau, still going at a high rate of speed they hit the base of the ramp. Up and off they sailed—into space. The last I saw of Ruth was her blonde hair standing out straight behind her.

Mama and Papa reached the side porch in time to see this metal magic carpet flying by with their daughter riding the tail.

When it lost speed, it descended rapidly. It landed, as planned, in Hagar's yard. It glided on the ground only a short distance before coming to a stop. (Which was a good thing because Ruth wrapped her fingers around the tin to hold on and her mittens were torn and her fingers cut and bruised when it rolled along the ground—something she didn't mention to Mama and Papa.)

"It was great! It worked just like we thought it would," the engineers shouted as we joined them at the landing spot. Their eyes sparkled like candles on a Christmas tree as they told how it felt to sail through the air.

"Can I go next?" "I want to go next!" everyone was shouting for a turn.

But it wasn't to be because Papa arrived at the scene.

"You could cut your head off on that deathtrap!" he screamed as he grabbed Ruth and held her tight. Other parents came and that spelled doom for the tin toboggan. The maiden voyage was its first and last, much to the disappointment of the kids who didn't have a turn.

Still, Ruth had her ride in the sky. Parental disapproval didn't faze her any more than the flight. Furthermore, she didn't even seem to notice that the other kids were pretty envious, especially her younger sister.

That night Mama had a serious talk with Papa. "Bill, why

don't you buy a house so we can get out of this neighborhood before something happens to one of the kids? You know very well that it's no place to raise children."

As usual, Papa didn't pay much attention. He grunted a few responses until she finally gave up. Rod, Ruth and I looked at one another unable to understand why Mama would feel that way about my Monterey.

In our neighborhood was another special home built sled put together by Les McGill and some of the other older boys. The front was a regular sled with swivel bars for steering and the back was a stationery sled. In between, they put a plank that held seven or eight people. After pulling their bobsled to the top of Center Avenue Hill, they climbed aboard. A couple fellows gave them a big push and they were off, gliding down the hill, across Western Avenue, on over the bridge to the railroad track.

"It was a breathtaking ride. We didn't have to worry about any traffic but we were scared about hitting a train." Les told us. "It was sure a lot of fun."

What wasn't so much fun was pulling the heavy contraption back up the long hill. "But it was worth it for the fast ride down." he said.

The real bobsleds appeared when farmers replaced the wheels on their wagons with wide runners for snow covered roads. Other farmers had wagons permanently equipped with the bobsled runners. As the horses trotted along pulling the wagons filled with big cans of milk headed for the condensery, we liked to jump on the wide runners to hitch a ride. They were wide enough so it was comfortable, not like the cutters on the sleighs. Often times, the older boys tied their sleds to the bobsleds. Sometimes they got a faster and more dangerous ride than they bargained for when the farmer whipped the horses and turned the corners going lickety split.

The hills and roads weren't the only places for action in the winter. When the river froze over by the Big Rock, it became a gathering place for kids of all ages. I liked to watch them play hockey but was careful to get out of the way when the puck came my way. They didn't have money to buy a real puck so they used a round, flat can which scarred up the faces of many a player. One of the younger kids, Buddy Schumacher, skated like a little demon carrying a hockey stick that towered over his head.

Our folks were always afraid we would fall through the ice so Ruth, Rod and I didn't get to skate. One night after I teased and teased Papa to take me skating, he took me down to the Big Rock. He clamped on the ice skates and when I wobbled toward the ice he tied a rope around my waist so he could pull me out if I fell in.

After that experience I went back to being a spectator. Hugo Preuss, one of the older fellows, was the star performer with his long graceful strides, grapevine turns, jumps and spins. At times, he selected a partner, who looked great spinning across the ice in his arms.

It was near the Big Rock that ice was harvested and stored in the warehouse along the shore. We watched the workers make marks on the ice, etching it for the proper size. Then came the cutters to saw through the ice following the markings. A channel was cleared so that the chunks of ice could be floated to the ice house. Horses pulled the rope on the pulley that hauled the big chunks of ice up the chute. On occasion, a huge chunk would come loose and start sliding back down the chute. The workers shouted warnings and the spectators screamed as they skidded along the frozen river to get out of the way.

On days when the snow was fresh and white, we liked to lie on our backs in the fluffy white stuff and move our arms up and down to make an impression of an angel. But, we knew in a few days it would all be covered with black soot. Most everyone burned soft coal in their stoves. We did too except we used hard coal in the isinglass stove in the parlor. Chimneys in the neighborhood poured out the black smoke as did the trains as they went chugging by.

Maybe that's why we welcomed every snowfall; the drab and grungy winter landscape became bright and beautiful.

Chapter 22

Clarence

"Margie, for Heaven's sake tie your shoe laces. Why do you go around like that?" Clarence asked scathingly as we were leaving to attend a concert at the School for the Blind.

I flinched. I felt my face getting red. I resented his remark. I had heard it often enough from Mama, followed by "One of these days, you're going to trip and break your neck."

I knew it was a sloppy habit but what really upset me was to be scolded by Clarence. I wondered how he knew because he was blind. He was a student at the Blind School and tonight he was to play a violin solo.

Whenever he was to perform, his mother, a friend of Mama's, came from northern Wisconsin to stay with us for a few days. This was the first time we kids were told we would attend and I was not anxious to go.

I thought I had endured enough violin squawking without attending the concert. Mama loved the violin and insisted that my sister take lessons. Ruth's rendition of "Believe Me In all Those Endearing Young Charms" was worse than chalk squeaking on the blackboard.

"If she doesn't improve fast, and I mean FAST, we're going to call a halt to the lessons," Papa issued an ultimatum. Ruth didn't like taking lessons and the squawking got worse and worse. The lessons stopped. Only Mama was disappointed.

Anyway, I thought tying my laces was a big price to pay to go hear a concert I didn't want to hear. Clarence picked up his violin case and we were on our way.

The auditorium was packed with students, parents and townspeople as the musicians were warming up. The stage was decorated with big palms and baskets of flowers.

In spite of my reluctance to go, I really enjoyed the concert. Choral groups sang familiar songs in harmony, in parts, even in rounds. The orchestra played beautifully and the solo by Clarence made me aware of how a violin could sound in the hands of an accomplished musician. I was impressed.

If I was impressed, you can imagine how Clarence's mother was feeling. She sat tall in her seat, nodding her head to the beat of the music, beaming from ear to ear.

On the way home, Rod and I walked behind the others. Clarence stayed at the school. "I wonder if the blind have natural musical ability, or if they develop a keener sense of hearing, an ear for music, because they can't see?" I said.

Rod said he didn't know.

"Maybe that would explain why Clarence could hear my laces flopping," I said. "Anyway, he sure played well."

Later that evening we were all sitting around the dining room table and Clarence's mother was bubbling over with talk of the concert. She not only praised her son but also the teachers for the fine training and encouragement, and the institution that made it possible for her blind son to get an education and become self sufficient.

"When I told my neighbor on the next farm that we were sending Clarence to the school, she couldn't understand what for." The neighbor said "He's blind, what good will it do?" I went home and stewed and cried about it. I wanted to tell her that because he was blind did not mean he was stupid," she said. "You did the right thing sending him to school. It was back in about 1850, under the leadership of Captain Ira Miltimore and Josiah Willard, a group of residents met at a public hearing at the court house to determine what could be done to establish a school for the blind. Enough money was raised that night to get started," Papa recalled. "It was the first one in Wisconsin."

"I understand the first classes were held in a home owned

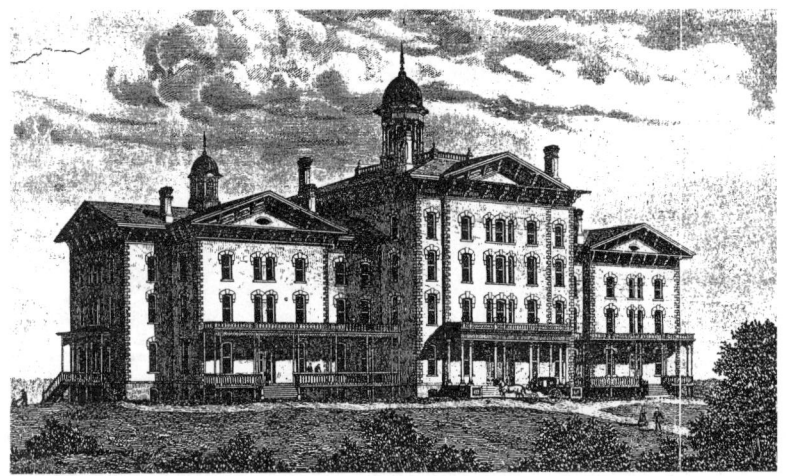

Clarence attended the School for the Blind which was organized under the leadership of Ira Miltimore and Josiah Willard in 1850. It was the first school for the blind in the state of Wisconsin.

by Mr. Miltimore and that he later donated the land where the school is located," Clarence's mother said.

"At first they stressed broom making and basket weaving but that has changed," she added and then talked about her son learning to read with his fingers, and about classes in arithmetic, geography, grammar, history and music.

"None of this training would have been possible if it hadn't been for people who thought not only of themselves but cared about others less fortunate," she said wiping a tear from her eyes.

"Was Clarence always blind?" I asked.

Mama glared at me. I realized I shouldn't have asked.

"You don't have to talk about it," Mama interrupted.

"Thank you, Carrie, it's been a wonderful day but I am tired and I think I'll go to bed," she replied.

After she went upstairs, Mama reminded me that I had upset her and that I shouldn't have asked. Later, Papa explained that Clarence was born in 1910, a year after the state passed a law to prevent blindness in babies by dropping a solution of silver nitrate in their eyes.

"Unfortunately, the mid-wife who helped with the delivery didn't know about it. This law has saved the sight of hundreds of other infants, but Clarence was not one of them."

I shuddered, wondering what it would be like not to see. I shut my eyes and groped my way to the stairway and up to bed. I thought about Clarence; how smart he was and how well he played the violin.

After Clarence graduated, we didn't see him or his mother again. But Mama received a letter from his proud mother, "Clarence has rented an apartment in town. He is teaching music and tuning pianos and plays with an orchestra. He is happy."

And I turned over a new leaf. I decided if it bothered a blind person, who could only hear the laces, that it must be even worse for those who could also see them. I no longer run around with flopping laces.

Chapter 23

A 'Miss Popularity' Contest

"Carrie, you're not going to believe this—the railroad men picked an old hag who lives in a shack by the railroad tracks as their candidate for 'Miss Popularity'." Papa's eyes sparkled as he walked in the door, took the *Janesville Gazette* from under his arm, and tossed it on the kitchen table. He sat down and pushed out a chair for Mama.

As Mama seldom went out of the house except to pump water, hang up washing, or play with us kids, she eagerly awaited Papa's home coming to learn what was going on in the outside world. She enjoyed his graphic version of the news as he detailed, and perhaps exaggerated, the gossip and goings-on of prominent, and not so prominent, townspeople. Although we didn't sit at the table with them, Rod, Ruth and I were seldom out of earshot. Papa was superintendent at the Haskins, Schwartz Tobacco warehouse located near the Five Points, where he picked up a lot of his news, especially from the railroad workers.

"They've come up with a most unlikely contender for the honor of being Southern Wisconsin's most popular girl," Papa laughed as he unfolded the paper to show Mama the full page ad announcing the rules of the contest being held in connection with the opening of the new $250,000 Jeffris Theatre. In the ad was a listing of sponsors who were giving a ballot for every fifty cent purchase. First prize was to be one hundred gold dollars plus the honor of riding in the gala theatre opening parade with other contestants and dignitaries.

Mama looked up from the paper, "You don't think Lula has a chance to win, do you?"

"We'll have to wait and see. The railroad men are pretty determined. They say some of the Big Shots have favorite candidates and now they have their own favorite. They're sure having a lot of fun with it."

"I saw her today. I saw Lula," Papa shouted as he rushed in the door a few days later. "One of the railroad men waved to me to come out on the tracks so I could see her. She was hunching her way along the tracks picking up coal."

"When a train screeched by, Lula dropped her gunny sack and pushed back some straggles of hair under her bandanna, adding more soot to her grimy face. From cab to caboose, the railroad men leaned out of the train waving and shouting, LULA, LULA, LULA!"

"What did Lula do?" Mama asked.

"She grinned from ear to ear. She waved both arms and took several deep bows. She loved it."

"But, you don't think she can win, do you?" Mama asked, "the Gazette shows she only has 4,000 votes and the top contestant has 60,000."

"That's going to change soon." A smug smile crossed Papa's face as he explained, "The railroad workers are holding back their ballots."

Although the *Gazette* reported nothing about Lula's campaign except in the tabulation, word spread like wildfire. Notwithstanding the national furor over the Leopold-Loeb murder case and the upcoming presidential election that Senator Bob LaFollette said he would win, in the Janesville area the Popularity Contest was the major topic of discussion.

On September 24, 1924, the tabulation showed Lula still had only 4,000 votes while the top vote-getter had 78,000. There was also another full page ad about the contest along with this editorial comment,

> 'with the contest to select the most popular girl in Southern Wisconsin rapidly nearing its final stretch, increased efforts are being exerted by the candidates to collect as many votes as possible for the big finish.'

Even though Lula's campaign was the talk of the town, the newspaper still didn't acknowledge it.

"The grapevine says Lula is gaining and it's getting the Big Shots' goat. They are more determined than ever to keep Lula from winning." We could tell Papa was relishing the controversy as he continued," other contestants are up in arms with this twist to the race. Some are dropping out and parents of the young ladies are writing letters to the editor complaining about the ridicule their daughters are enduring."

"That's all well and good, but, it's the 25th and there's only a few days left," Mama said as she showed Papa the paper, "Lula still has only 4,000 votes while the top contestant has 123,100." "Just wait and see." Papa seemed to be sure who was going to win. "In the next couple days the railroad workers will be going all over town depositing Lula's votes in the ballot boxes."

With the contest reaching a fever pitch, participating merchants and banks were doing a land office business. They ran several more advertisements including a double spread on September 27th,

> " Contest Ends September 30."
> "BUY YOUR CHRISTMAS GIFTS NOW'.

The night this ad appeared was the day Mary Lula Lee took the lead. The tabulation showed Lula had 288,800 votes. Pictures of the next three leading contestants ran with the story—but, again, no mention of Lula except in the tabulation. The article went on to say, 'There's a wild scramble for votes with only a few days left.'

"She did it. She's in the lead," Mama exclaimed as she pointed out the article to Papa.

"Yeah, it's getting wild and y'know it's the merchants and bankers who are reaping the benefits."

With the interest in the contest and the closeness of the race, the *Gazette* apparently wanted to make certain the contest was handled fair and square. They ran an ad announcing "the contest will end at 6 pm, September 30, at which time no more ballots will be given out. The ballot boxes at the four banks will be closed October 1, at 3 pm, upon closing of the banks. The *Gazette* office will remain open until 9 pm for late voters. Winners will be announced on October 2."

The eagerly-awaited edition carried the news,

'Mrs. Lee wins Popularity Contest with 1,900,000 votes, Rose Mills in second place with 1,807,300.' Mama held the paper in the air and marched around the room.

"They cooled down the ruffled feathers of the other contestants by coming up with additional prizes so they would agree to appear in the parade if Lula won," Papa said.

"What time is this grandiose parade going to start?" Mama asked as they read the details of plans for Lula's grand appearance, "this is something I don't want to miss."

In the meantime, although it was the railroad men who got Lula elected, it fell to their wives to get Lula ready for her role in the grand opening. It was not an easy task.

"Lula bellowed like a stuck pig when they pushed her in the tub to scrub her," Papa said as he came running in the door to tell Mama yet another Lula tale. "They thought they'd never get through the many layers of soot. They used a brush and kept changing the bath water. She fought like a tiger when they shampooed her hair but the women kept right at it determined to make her presentable.

On Saturday night, Papa, Mama and us kids joined the more than 20,000 people who lined the downtown streets to catch a glimpse of Lula. Helping to swell the crowd were hundreds of out-of-town railroad workers, from up and down the line, who had been following the contest.

The October 6, 1924, edition of the *Janesville Gazette* tells it best with a story that started on the front page. Papa and

Mama took turns reading it aloud.

20,000 CHEER FOR MISS POPULARITY IN NOVEL PARADE

HUSBAND OF WINNER ALSO GIVEN OVATION BY CROWD

IS GREAT EVENT

Demonstration Marking Theater Opening Hailed Big Success

Janesville added a palace of entertainment to its long list of assets, Saturday night, when the beautiful $250,000 Jeffris Theater of the Saxe Bros. of Milwaukee, was formally opened with ceremonies that attracted a crowd variously estimated between 20,000 and 25,000.

An audience that rivalled that which witnessed the Harvest Festival parade two years ago, was packed into every available inch of space along Main and Milwaukee streets, and saw the parade that culminated in the theater's dedication.

The cynosure of all eyes, Mrs. Mary Lula Lee, 108 South Chatham street, enjoyed the happiest moment of her 67 years of a life filled with adversity, when she rode through the business district in regal splendor, amid the mingled strains of band music, the beat of drums, the cheers and laughter of thousands. All the honor befitting one who had been chosen "Southern Wisconsin's most popular girl" was accorded her.

Many Cities Represented.

Janesville has seen a few events that brought larger crowds, but none that attracted part of its audience from such a wide area, as that of Saturday night when a desire to see this elderly and poor woman, who had outdistanced a field of young persons in a popularity contest, drew them from many, far distant points, including Milwaukee, Elgin, Rockford, Beloit and Madison.

In the parade were the winners of the popularity contest, each riding in a separate car, they being Mrs. Lee and Misses Rose Mills, Jessie McGregor, Marjorie Cook and Bessie Ellis. Miss Alvina Feltz, winner of fourth place, and Miss Gladys Peterson, who finished sixth, did not participate.

Husband Cheered Too

Attracting as much attention as the winners, was Austin Lee, husband of "Miss Popularity." Attired in a high silk hat, blue denim shirt and Prince Albert coat, Mr. Lee was loudly cheered.

The crack St. John's Military Academy band of Delafield led the parade. Emerson Badgley, the drum major, directed the 29 pieces. Captain R. C. Jack and Principal W. W. Brown led the Janesville school bands with a combined strength of 150. The Parker Pen company band, Reuben Joseph, leader, was the third musical organization in the procession.

Arriving late, the 24-piece Milwaukee Elks bugle and drum corps, joined in the parade. They were led by Walter Ziege. Their presence here was a tribute to the popularity of the Saxe Bros. who are members.

Comedy in Parade

Held high above the 24 purple and white uniformed men, was a banner, saying, "Hello Janesville. Milwaukee Elks are proud of Saxe Bros. so we're your friends too."

The comedy for the parade was furnished by several floats, the largest of which was a hay rack upon which an orchestra played and carried a group of Mrs. Lee's large army of enthusiastic supporters.

Harry Mason rode a horse carrying a sign, "Budding daughters also ran," and the Cronin Dairy company showed a touch of humor, entering a pet goat upon a truck. Several other decorated automobiles were in the parade.

Crowd Gathers Early

The features were the crowd and Mrs. Lee. Seven o'clock, nearly two hours before the parade commenced, people took up their vigil along Main and Milwaukee streets to await the approach of the column. They started on the sidewalk and overflowed into the middle of the street. Hundreds sat in cars parked in every available place.

Miles of cars were parked on the side streets. Some ingenuous persons parked their cars downtown early in the afternoon and left them there so that they might be sure to see the parade. Other *energetic people climbed to the tops of business blocks for a vantage point.*

When the parade started people lined the streets from the high school to Academy and Milwaukee street. From the corner of Court and Main to the Jeffris theater there was one solid mass of humanity. Traffic and business was at a standstill. Pedestrians could not move. Several women fainted.

Mrs. Lee Modestly Attired.

Mrs. Lee was simply attired in a modest brown silk dress, and wore high black shoes. Upon her head, she wore a crown of gold leaves and roses. Her only adornment of jewelry was a necklace and a cameo pin upon her breast.

The little woman was not slow to give expression to her ecstasy, produced by the cheers of the multitude, only a small portion of which two weeks ago had known she existed in Janesville as she has for 18 years. Almost incessantly, she waved handkerchiefs held in each hand, in reply to greeting from the audience. She bowed to some, who familiarly called her by name.

In front of the Jeffris theater, Mrs. Lee was assisted to a standing position atop the rear seat of her car by Thomas Saxe and she waved and bowed to the greetings. After a short introductory speech, the procession moved to the five points where it disbanded, the winning contestants being taken to the theater.

An expected audience that packed the theater waited to the close of the first show, when the curtains parted to disclose Mrs. Lee, seated in a lattice covered throne, with the four young women on each side.

Elk Ruler Introduced.

M. G. Jeffris, Janesville attorney, introduced Chauncey Yockey, Milwaukee, exalted ruler of Milwaukee Elks, who, after a short speech praising the theater and the enterprise of the Saxe Bros. introduced Pat Kelly, another Milwaukean, who eulogized the two Milwaukee theater proprietors.

"The queen, Mrs. Mary Lula Lee, wins the honors of first place," said Mr. Yockey, "so come forth, Mary Lula Lee, and receive the award you have received at the efforts of your many friends in this

community."

"Yes, and I want to thank my many friends for what they have done for me," said Mrs. Lee in her curtain speech, as she was presented with her prizes, the $100 in gold, a gold life pass to the theater and an additional $10.

Miss Rose Mills, whose showing in coming within 92,501 votes of winning the contest was recognized by Saxe Bros. in similar prizes, was presented. The prizes for other contestants were given them amid applause.

Mrs. Lee, with her husband, Austin was presented again to the audience at the close of the second show. Eddie Steed introducing the couple.

The opening of the Jeffris, giving Janesville four theaters, was crowned with success as attends few private enterprises.

Saxe Officials Here

Members of the Saxe Bros. organization, here for the opening, included the following: Alford Gillickson, Modjeska theater; manager of the Rialto and Princess theaters, Milwaukee; John Keough, general booking manager; Charles Brewster, superintendent of maintenance, Ed Wiesfelt, stage presentation manager, M. R. Salter, auditor; John Strais, assistant auditor.

Many large floral baskets lined the rear of the theater, bringing messages of congratulation to the Saxe Bros. They were from the following: Film Board of Trade, Milwaukee, T. M. Ellis, Beloit theater proprietor; Schueppert Printing company, The Exhibitors Supply Co., Walter Schroeder, Lyman Ballant of the United Artists, C. Wallace and A. J. Wooden, Milwaukee, Golden Eagle, MecNeil Hotel company and A. S. Hegg of Janesville.

Both Thomas and John Saxe were here for the opening of their newest theater and were pleased by the reception on the first night.

Buys First Ticket

The theater opened at 6:40 p.m. and John Heller of 309 South Franklin street had the honor of buying the first ticket. Mr. Heller helped install the steam fitting.

The uniformed doorman in blue and the ushers in mulberry and beige lend an atmosphere to the theater that Janesville has not *previously enjoyed. The ushers are: Joe Stead, chief; John Haupt, Ray McCue, Howard McGowan, John Klenatz and Clarence Govel. Elva Rashid is in the ticket booth and John Allen is doorman. J. L. Morrissey is the manager and R. L. Hoenick, assistant manager.*

Week-end Program Good

There may be nothing new on earth but there are many things which are new to Janesville and the Jeffris theater week-end program was a revelation to local theater-goers. Novelty of presentation and a keen appreciation of nicety in details marked the entire bill.

Two popular movie stars, Colleen Moore and Conway Tearle, in "Flirting With Love" lent much as the headline attraction. A pen and ink vaudeville comedy balanced the moving picture contribution to the program.

Stage presentations and organ recitals which are of metropolitan vogue will be features of each program. The week end stage presentation was "In a Rose Bower, an artistic and lovely number presented amid a bower of roses. Miss Merle Spangenburg, Milwaukee, as the soloist sang "Love Sends a Little Gift of Roses," and two young women, pupils of the Abbott school of dancing, Chicago, gave a dance number. With hooped skirts, pastel shades of taffeta, lace pantaloons and old fashioned bonnets, enhanced by a background of roses, a truly aesthetic effect was produced.

The organ accompaniment for the entire program added much to the enjoyment of the entertainment. Alfred Dullechsen, the boy wonder of Chicago, will be the regular organist at the theater.

Papa put down the paper. Reaching over to take Mama's hand, he said, "Y'know Carrie, Lula and her husband were treated with consideration and respect. This was a great contest, one we will never forget. And, Lula and the railroad men deserve a lot of credit. In spite of the hullabaloo, I believe Lula brought our community closer together."

Chapter 24

Our Mean Streak

As I mentioned before, Mama didn't go out much. I think that's why she was happy to feed the hoboes and tramps, and why she welcomed door-to-door salespeople, especially the Larkin Lady who stopped regularly.

On this rainy morning, Mrs. Curler arrived with her daughter, Esther. She rapped loudly at the front door, shook out her big black umbrella, folded it and left it on the porch. As soon as Mama let her in and they sat down at the dining room table, Mrs. Curler opened her black leatherette case containing literature on products, such as spices and vanilla, along with a list of prizes and order blanks. The prizes, given for purchasing a certain amount of merchandise, were mostly decorative items like a tall glass water pitcher, etched glass vase with curved handles, candlesticks or fancy bowls. These prizes were Mama's pride and joy.

While the Larkin Lady and Mama got down to business, the little girl sat near them at the table looking at a magazine Mama gave her. Ida, Ruth Thom, and my sister and brother and I were in the front room reading poetry out loud.

Often on a rainy day, Ida would say, "Let's go to your house and read poetry." Mama let us use the front room where the books were, a room usually closed off and used only on Sunday nights or for special company.

In her best dramatic fashion, Ida was half reading and half reciting *The Raven* by Edgar Allan Poe.

Once upon a midnight dreary, while I pondered weak and weary,
Over many a quaint and curious volume of forgotten lore,
While I nodded, nearly napping, suddenly there came a tapping
As of someone gently rapping, rapping at my chamber door.
"Tis some visitor," I muttered, "tapping at my chamber door— Only this and nothing more."

The intensity and hypnotic flow of the words commanded our full attention. At a verse ending with, "quoth the raven nevermore," Ida signalled for all of us to repeat, "quoth the raven nevermore," which we did in a somber, dreary fashion. Followed by laughter.

Ruth Thom read *Annabel Lee*. My sister read *The Curfew Must not Ring Tonight* using the tieback on the curtain to pretend she was swinging out over the city, holding on to the clapper to keep the bell from ringing, thus saving her lover's life.

I recited one of Papa's favorite poems, *The End of a Perfect Day*. When he was in school, kids memorized a lot of poetry. He could still recite many long poems, which he often did on Sunday nights as we gathered around the brightly burning isinglass stove in the front room.

We read, in a loud and dramatic fashion, the well known literary works of the great English authors. The more melancholy the verse, the more we giggled. Yet, in our own way, enjoying the words of the famous poets.

In the next room, Mama noticed the Larkin Lady was getting nervous. Her face was tight as she leaned over and asked Mama, "Are those kids making fun of me?"

We really weren't. We forgot she was there but Mama wasn't sure because sometimes we could be mean.

For one thing, we delighted in picking on Kate, the widow lady, across the street; jumping on her porch at night or knocking on the door and running off. When we saw her outside in the yard, we'd sing/shout "K-K-K-Kate, Beautiful

Kate" at the top of our lungs. On the other hand, when any of us were alone, we would greet her politely, "How are you today, Mrs. Bergher?" I guess there must be some truth in the 'dogs in a pack' theory.

Another of our mean tricks was to watch for the three sisters who lived past the arch to come by. They were always dressed up and "smarty-acting" we thought. We'd run upstairs in our barn that was right next to the walkway, gather up bits of hay and dirt, and sprinkle it down on them. The uppity sisters became very agitated as they tried to brush off the itchy, sticky stuff from themselves and from one another. We howled with laughter as we watched their contortions as they hurried down the street, wriggling and dusting, like they were having fits.

By far more dangerous, was the habit of the older boys throwing rocks at people from atop the railroad bank. They supposedly aimed at the ground close to us. The rocks landed near our feet, sending the dust flying, and sometimes bouncing up and hitting us in the legs. It hurt, usually making black and blue marks, but it was all part of the game.

One day Ruth Thom and I were running for cover at her house to get away from the rock throwers, when a rock hit her in the right temple. She dropped to the ground in a heap, unconscious. I thought she was dead. We carried her limp body into her house. Her face was white as chalk and her skin looked thin as paper stretched over her face. Mrs. Thom called the doctor.

"It was a close call but she should be all right. Just keep her quiet for a few days. I'll leave some pills because her head is going to ache for a while," the Doctor said as he gave Mrs. Thom the pills.

We knew the brothers who threw the rocks. They were really friends and we liked them, so there was nothing personal about the attack—except on that day, for some unknown reason, we wouldn't let them join us in making Mulligan stew.

The boys' father came over to see how Ruth was doing. The boys told him they were afraid they had killed her. The father, obviously relieved to learn she would be all right, offered to pay the doctor bill.

"And I'll teach my boys a lesson they won't forget," he added, fingering his leather belt. I don't think those kids ever threw any more rocks, probably because of the scare, not the licking.

Of course, we could be mean to each other too. Like the time my sister was miffed at Ida. Ruth knew Ida was scared to death of snakes so she found a good-sized garter snake which she held behind her back as she hurried over to Huber's.

"Ida, Ida, come out and play," she yelled.

When Ida opened the door, Ruth threw the wiggly, live snake hitting her in the face. Ida flew into a real tizzy.

To get even, Ida made up a bunch of mud balls, came over to our house and called for Ruth. When Ruth opened the door, Ida slung the mud balls at her. However, Ruth was expecting the visit and she quickly jumped to one side. The mud balls hit the new wallpaper in the dining room. Mama jumped up.

"That Ida. What will she do next? That was totally unprovoked. Ruth was just sitting here reading. I'm going to tell her mother," Mama exploded.

Ruth's eyes sparkled and she rubbed her hands together at the prospect of getting Ida in more trouble. I knew I should probably tell Mama about Ruth throwing the snake, but, I thought if I waited a while, Rod would tell her. But neither of us did.

Mama usually held us three blameless no matter what happened. Papa, on the other hand, would have asked Ruth why Ida threw the mud balls. And, Ruth would tell him the truth. We always told the truth, however, sometimes we felt it was important not to volunteer information. We appreciated Mama taking our part, even when we knew it wasn't fair.

The next day, after Mrs. Huber had cleaned off the wallpaper, we were friends again. But Ida couldn't help getting in the last word.

"It was all your fault, Ruth. You know it was all your fault. You shouldn't have jumped out of the way!" she yelled.

But, on that day when we were reading poetry, we really weren't making fun of the Larkin Lady. But, she thought we were. Mama tried to tell her we always acted that way. She didn't believe her. She finished writing the order and quickly left the house—leaving her daughter and umbrella behind.

"Where is my Mama? When will she be back?" the little girl asked.

"She will miss you in a little while, Esther, and she'll be back," Mama assured her.

The time passed slowly for the little girl and she started to cry. Mother kept watching for her mother. In about a half hour, she saw her hurrying toward our house.

Mama opened the door as she approached but before she could say a word the Larkin Lady said,

"I forgot my umbrella so I came back to get it." She quickly grabbed it and started back off the porch.

Mama's mouth dropped open. "Wait a minute. Wait a minute, what about Esther?"

After they were gone, Mama came storming in the front room.

"Do you know what you've done? You got that nice Mrs. Curler so upset that she forgot her daughter!"

She ordered Ida and Ruth Thom to go home. (Knowing Mama, she probably thought it was all Ida's fault.)

"But Mama," I started to protest that it wasn't fair. Then I remembered it wasn't fair not to tell Mama about Ruth throwing the snake at Ida, or dropping dirt on the nice Havlicek sisters who never did anything to us. And, it wasn't fair that Ruth Thom got hit by the stone because she never threw a stone in her life or started any trouble. And, it wasn't fair that Mrs. Curler thought we were making fun of her when we really weren't.

"What's fair and what isn't fair?" I wondered. "Is there justice, or do things somehow equal out?"

Chapter 25

The Stork Hoax

"I have some really big news to tell you tonight, but I can't tell you if any of the boys are there," Ida said in her mysterious, yet know-it-all manner.

Right at dusk, my sister and I were there, eagerly awaiting whatever news Ida had in mind for us. Other neighborhood girls soon joined us, also curious, yet uneasy wondering why the boys weren't invited. We didn't talk as we huddled together on the platform rock in front of our house, our regular meeting place, waiting for Ida.

The corner street light, a single bulb hanging from a long wire, managed a weak circle of light just beyond where we waited allowing enough darkness to share confidences with ease. It was here that Ida, who was a few years older, shared her worldly knowledge. Some was fact and some was fiction; I never knew for sure which was which but it didn't make any difference—the stories she made up were fun too.

"Before we start, do you swear on a stack of Bibles you won't tell?" Ida asked as soon as she joined us. She looked from one to another. We all nodded. "You promise?" She waited until each of us made a verbal promise.

"Do you know where babies come from?" she asked in a low voice as she leaned forward.

I thought that was a silly question. Of course we knew. Mama told us that storks delivered the babies. Everyone knew that. We nodded vigorously to let Ida know we knew about babies.

"You don't believe that bunk about the storks bringing the babies, do you?" She squinted as she looked from face to face in the near darkness.

Dead silence. Of course we believed it.

"My aunt told me the doctor brings the baby in his black bag," one girl whispered.

"That's a lot of bunk, too," Ida said, "Remember, you promised not to tell." As an extra precaution, Ida insisted we all repeat the "criss-cross my heart, I hope to die" routine.

"Do you really want to know where babies come from? she asked in a slow hushed whisper. We wiggled uncomfortably but nodded.

Ida bent down not looking at us, as she confided under her breath, "they grow in your mother's belly and come out her bottom."

My friend Ruth Thom put her hand over her mouth to keep from throwing up and ran for home. My sister and I rushed in the house, past Mama and Papa, and up to bed.

As I was going up the steps I heard Mama say to Papa, "Did you see their faces? Ida must have told them another of those wild ghost story."

My sister and I didn't talk about it. The idea was too upsetting. I was glad to get in bed and pull the covers up over my head. I was sure Ida was lying. It was another of her made-up tales. I was nine years old; I believed what Mama told me—that the stork brings the babies.

I didn't want to believe Ida. I remembered I didn't want to believe her when she told us about Santa Claus—and how angry Mama was when we told her. Later, we learned Ida was telling the truth. Was it possible she was telling the truth now? I tossed and turned.

After a restless night, I awoke the next morning still thinking of what Ida had told us. I met a classmate on the way to school and as we walked along my thoughts were on the news Ida had given us. Even though I still didn't believe Ida's story, and even though I had sworn on a stack of Bibles and criss-crossed my heart not to tell, I blurted out the awful story.

Lorraine's eyes popped wide open. She turned stark white and stopped in her tracks. I thought she was going to throw up. She turned around as though she was going back home, then turned back and went on to school. She didn't say a word, just gave me a dirty look.

That night when I got home from school, my classmate's mother was at our door talking to Mama. I knew I was in trouble when I saw the way her head was shaking and her arms waving in Mama's face.

"Shame on you, shame on you!" Mama shouted the minute she saw me. She lunged out the door and down the porch steps, sliding one forefinger over the other, "Shame! Shame on you!" "Why would you talk of such things?"

"Don't you ever speak to Lorraine again," my classmate's mother said with a sneer. She gave me a look of total disgust, as she lifted her head, all high and mighty, and stalked out of the yard.

My face burned. I cringed. I felt dirty all over. Mama's face was a ghastly shade of green, her blue eyes filled with alarm, even hatred, as she continued the awful gesturing.

"Shame on you. How could you? Go to your room and stay there till supper," she spat out.

I was glad to get to my bedroom. No one, especially Mama, had ever treated me that way before. I always felt loved and secure. Now I didn't know what to think or what to believe. Was what Ida told us true? Why couldn't I ask Mama if it was? Why didn't she tell me? Ida's news must be true. If not, why would Mama be so upset? Why had Mama lied to me? I decided the truth about where babies come from must be very bad. So bad, that no one could talk about it.

Now that I knew the truth, did it make me bad? A shameful person? Would I be shunned by all my classmates? What had I done? Did this knowledge change me? Was I no longer an innocent child because I KNEW?

It didn't take Mama long to figure out where I got my information. In our neighborhood, no matter what happened, it was always Ida who got the blame. The fact that "it was all

Ida's fault" was supposed to take some of the guilt away from me—but it didn't.

Ida hadn't told us, and maybe didn't know, how the babies got in the mother's stomach. We didn't even wonder about it. And, of course, nobody talked about it.

That is, until a couple years later when I took a note home from Jr. High school asking for Mama's permission to attend a meeting for girls only, where a visiting nurse would explain menstruation. I was allowed to attend although many of the girls couldn't because their parents wouldn't sign the slip.

It was awkward and embarrassing as the nurse approached the subject, trying to explain how privileged we were to be female, and then the process. One classmate fainted and had to be taken to the office. The rest of us squirmed and waited for it to be over. It was the first time I had heard of the monthly period. Most girls learned about it when they suddenly started bleeding. They didn't know what was wrong. Many thought they were dying. Even older sisters didn't "tell" younger sisters to prepare them. I guess that was why schools held the class.

At least I knew what was happening when a couple years later I started to spot. I asked my sister what to do and she showed me where the rags were kept and the sanitary belt along with the big safety pins. She also pointed out the pail for the soiled rags telling me, "You have to wash them yourself."

The rags were old pieces of toweling or sheets to be folded over and pinned to a belt. They were bulky, uncomfortable and could only be changed at home. At school, especially on warm days, we could usually tell who was having their period by the odor surrounding them.

To me, everything about it was bad. I was afraid to move for fear the stains would show through my clothing. And, I couldn't go swimming. Then the awful chore of washing out the rags. When I removed them (not an easy task), I put them to soak in a covered pail of cold water. Using hot sudsy water and a washboard, I scrubbed and scrubbed. Even so, it was messy and hard to get them clean.

"Hang them outside on the line. The sun will bleach the stains and make them sanitary," Mama said. These were the only words she ever uttered about you know what.

Seeing the ugly, frayed rags waving in the sunlight seemed shameful, an admission to being a part of an untalked-about, degrading scheme, inflicted only on women.

Later, we learned of a new product, Kotex. Much as we appreciated the convenience and comfort, my sister and I always argued about who would go into the drug store to buy it. Uncomfortable and red-faced, we usually ended up going in together, hoping the clerk was no one we knew.

All this, and I still didn't know how babies got started. A friend said it was from kissing and I believed her. But then, once again, the schools came through to offer information with a session, for girls only, on "the birds and the bees". Mama signed the consent slip and handed it to me without looking at me.

The nurse was pleasant and relaxed. She told us of the reproductive system in a casual manner using diagrams. In conclusion, she explained it was "God's way to replenish the earth. . . a wonderful, natural system for man, animals, and the birds and the bees."

"Are there any questions?," she asked at the end of the meeting, looking around the room at the white faces.

I wanted to ask, "If this is such a wonderful, natural process, why can't people talk about it? Why don't our parents want us to know about it? What is so awful about it?"

But I didn't ask. No one else asked any questions either.

I had learned my lesson. Even though what Ida told us was true, it's something you don't talk about.

Chapter 26

Diving Off The Bridge
The Monterey Dam

The pounding of the dam banged in my ears. I was scared. I felt its pulsating strength, vitality and energy—its very own heartbeat. I was awed. The powerful Monterey Dam possessed a magnetism that pulled us back, again and again. It was the core of Monterey, the center of our universe. It became our lodestone compelling us to touch base almost against our will. At first we were content to sit alongside the dam on the big platform rock with giant steps, frightened to be that close to the powerful rush of water, splashing, tumbling and churning. We couldn't take our eyes off the bouncing water as its color changed from shades of green and blue to white. The raging stream roared. It sent sprays of cold mist, cooling our faces, reminding us of its force. We wondered aloud where all the water was coming from and where it was going. We listened to its music and rhythm challenging us, daring us to test its power. We're driven to accept the challenge—not in disrespect—but because of our great respect. We knew we were flirting with danger.

At first, we threw sticks in the river above the dam watching them cavort, down and around, up and down, finally working their way out of the tumult to continue bobbing downstream. On days when no water was flowing over the dam, we sat on it, watching the fishermen and waving at the trainmen as the trains roared over the railroad trestle.

The Monterey Dam (recent photo)

When only a little water was flowing over the dam, we made our way cautiously, and slowly, across the mossy, slippery crest careful not to fall in the water and rocks below. As we became braver, we ran across it fearlessly.

We watched the older kids respond to the dam's challenge, testing its power by slipping under it. We wanted to join them. I grabbed Ida's hand. She pulled me in that wondrous space under the dam, under its booming cascade. The colors from the inside were even more alive and colorful. The deafening noise of the water flying overhead prompted me to hold my hands over my ears.

I stood there with the other kids in what seemed like a secret hideaway. It was fun and exciting, yet, all I could think of was, "What would Mama say".

The Rock River and the dam attracted adults as well as kids. Young men and old, fished the waters of the Rock. We were fascinated as men caught turtles and wrestled them into a bucket, telling us, "They make good soup." We watched the hoboes walk to their camp under the railroad trestle. On hot days, in spite of the ragged, sharp rocks and strong current, girls and young women waded in the shallow area below the dam holding their skirts high as the water splashed around them. They sometimes waded across the river, when the water was low, to get colored sand from the limestone cliff on the left bank.

Although some of the kids swam in the area on the north side of the red iron Monterey Bridge, our favorite swimming hole was down river past the Woolen Mill at the "The Island". The water there wasn't as deep, there was no current and the river bed was mushy, not rocky.

The attraction to the dam could be fatal to those who went too far. Our friend Jake, Ida's brother, was one of the lucky ones to get out alive after going over the dam while it was running at full power. The firemen came, sirens going full force and lights flashing, but Jake made it out alone. He told me later, "I grabbed the rocks and pulled myself down stream toward the abutment as the water bashed me around." It was a frightening experience—even for one as fearless as Jake.

"When I went to bed, I kept hearing the roar of the dam. It kept wailing and wailing like it was mad because it didn't get me. I couldn't get to sleep," he said.

A favorite pastime of some of the bigger boys and young men was to jump, or dive, from the bridge. Some jumped at road level, others from the railing and the bravest climbed even higher to a criss cross in the bracing about half way up the bridge.

As Ruth and I watched them, I thought they were clumsy and awkward. "If they can do it, I can do it. And I can do it better," I said to Ruth. At the time I didn't think of the dam as being part of the challenge.

Several years later, when I was 13 or 14, I decided I was ready to take the leap. All the way to the bridge, my sister Ruth and our friend, Dorothy Buss, tried to talk me out of it. But I wouldn't listen.

They sat by the bank watching as I started climbing up on

After watching the fellows dive off the red iron Monterey Bridge, I decided I could do it better. I climbed up to the crossbars and dove in. I was lucky to survive.

the bridge railing, then on up to the superstructure, to the opening about five or ten feet above the railing. When I reached it, holding tight to the bridge, I straightened up and looked down. I was much higher than I thought I would be, probably 25 feet above the water. The river was a long, long, way down. I was scared. Then I saw the iron bracing parallel to the bridge and beyond that several rows of wires. I knew I had to dive between the bracing and the wires. Now I was really frightened. If I'd had any common sense I would have climbed down. But, I didn't.

(Years later I talked to another neighborhood girl, Evelyn Fairfield, who jumped from the road level of the bridge and landed flat on her back. She said, "I don't know what ever made me do it.")

Like Evelyn, I don't know what got into me, but I was determined. And I knew I had to act quickly before I lost my nerve. Like Ida always said, *"Don't think about it - just do it!"*

I took a deep breath, jumped up, arms outstretch, head back and legs arched in a swan dive, quickly straightening out in time to pass between the bracing and the wires. It was a long way down. I made a clean entry, legs together and toes pointed. In this streamline position I sank like a rock going deeper and deeper. I tried to raise my head and arms to break the entry and come to the surface but I couldn't get in the right position. I felt the cold, underwater current tugging at me. It seemed like a long time before I finally came up, gasping for air. It was then I heard the terrifying roar of the Monterey Dam over my shoulder. I knew I was in trouble.

I quickly went into a crawl stroke, using my strong flutter kick, as I stroked furiously for shore. When I came up for air, I saw I was still in the same place, not gaining on the dam. Keeping my head underwater, I took several strong strokes, kicking with all my might. When I lifted my arm and turned my head to suck in some air, I realized I wasn't gaining on the strong current. In a desperate effort, I lowered my head and stroked and kicked as hard and fast as I could. I was straining. I wondered how long I could keep this up.

Then I felt a hand on my arm firmly pulling me toward the bank. I kept kicking and stroking with my left hand to help. My rescuer pulled me at an angle downstream to avoid the full force of the current. When we reached the edge of the river, he pushed me onto the land. He then walked away without saying a word. He didn't even bawl me out for doing such a dumb thing.

I knew who he was. His name was Fred "Red" Sanstrom, who lived past the arch behind our house with his sister, Alma Maresch. He was one of the regulars who fished every day from the abutment under the bridge: men who often played the role of lifesavers.

I sat hugging my knees and shivering as Ruth and Dorothy ran over with my towel and my clothes.

"Are you all right? Are you O.K.?" they asked.

I nodded. I guess I was too grateful to be alive to be embarrassed. I dried off, dressed and we started for home. Dorothy didn't say anything as we walked along and neither did I. But I knew I could always count on Ruth to always have the last word.

"You do the dumbest things. You know that swan dive could of been your Swan Song—I hope you're satisfied!"

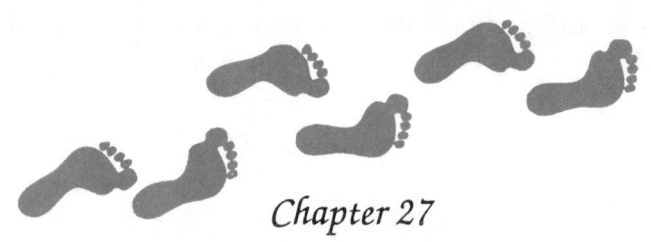

Chapter 27

Papa's Passing

One night after we finished eating supper, Papa said he had some news for us. Rod, Ruth and I gathered around him, anxious to hear what he had to tell us. "Next month we are moving to a nice house in a good neighborhood." It hit us like a thunderbolt.

"We have to move from Monterey?" We cried. We knew they had been looking at places but Ruth said Papa was doing it just to please Mama—that Papa would never make us move. We couldn't believe we had to leave our friends and our neighborhood.

Over the years, Mama kept suggesting they buy a house. But Papa was against it—always coming up with some reason, "It's too small" or "It's not the right neighborhood."

But now, we were really going to move. Papa rented a house on the corner of Mineral Point Avenue and Oakhill Avenue on the north west side of town. We said our good-bye's to friends and vowed we would keep in touch.

Mama loved the bright, cheery house and the neighborhood. Papa planted a big garden and Rod and I sold enough vegetables in the summer to pay the rent. We made new friends and walked to school with Gert Hansen, Rosie Miklos and Isabel Quaerna, but we kept in touch with Ida and the Thom's and Monterey. But all was not well.

Papa started losing weight. His pants were baggy on his lean frame. And, he rested a lot. He still went to work every day. Then one evening, less than a year since we'd moved, he told us we had to move to a house where the rent was cheaper. It was a dingy place on McKinley Street. We were ashamed of it and didn't want our school friends to know where we moved. But Rosie insisted so one day after school they came to see it. Much to our embarrassment. Mama never complained but we knew she hated to move.

About a month after we moved, Papa came home from work, plopped in a chair and said to Mama, "Carrie, I'm sorry I didn't buy a house so you and the kids could have a place to live if something happens to me." I was doing the dishes in the kitchen when I overheard his words. He sounded tired and sad. I wondered what he meant. I knew Papa had been doctoring and was not feeling well but I didn't think it was anything serious. A chill went through me.

Trembling, I peeked in the dining room and saw Mama and Papa sitting at the table. Papa's face was gray and haggard as he talked quietly to Mama who was resting her head in her hands as she leaned on the table.

"Carrie, I have come to the conclusion I have cancer," Papa confided to Mama in a grave voice.

I didn't know what cancer was: I never heard the word before. Yet I knew, from the tone of his voice, it was something terrible. A sense of foreboding flashed through me. I felt a sharp pain stab my stomach. I collapsed on the chair and held the dish towel to my face - unable to imagine what our lives would be like without Papa.

About a week later, Papa was too weak to go to work. Mama was doing the laundry. "Carrie, let me help you put up the clothes line," Papa said as he wearily lifted himself from his chair. He had never helped Mama with any of the housework before. He was awkward and clumsy as he tried to hold the rope. Mama assured him she could do it alone and he settled back in his chair. I wondered if he was feeling guilty for not helping Mama in the past. Now, when he wanted to help, he couldn't.

"Bill is nothing, but skin and bones," Aunt Mayme said when she came to visit. We were all worried about him.

Papa could no longer drag himself to work and was confined to his bed. Severe stomach cramps racked his body. He held tight to the bedstead, trying not to cry out. We took turns putting cold towels on his forehead.

One day he called for me. I grabbed a washcloth and dipped it in cool water from the basin to wipe the perspiration off his face. As I put the cloth on his hot skin, he took my hand. "Margie, I want you take good care of Mama. Promise me you will." He was distressed, uneasy. His voice trailed off.

I understood what was happening. Papa was dying and he's worried about Mama. A death-bed wish. I nodded even though I didn't know what an eleven year old would be able to do. I patted his hand, kissed him, and hurried from the room so he wouldn't see my tears.

The next day the he was admitted to Mercy Hospital, a Catholic hospital run by an order of nuns. The doctor said he had a bowel obstruction. He never mentioned cancer. They were able to give him medicine to relieve his pain.

"He is doing much better," the nun told us. "Go home, all of you, you need a good night's rest," she ordered.

We followed her instructions. We went to bed that night believing he would get better. But the next morning we were summoned to the hospital. Papa was dying. When we walked in his room, Mama told us to say good-bye to our father. Each of us kissed him. I felt a little squeeze on my hand so I knew he was still alive.

Then Mama leaned over and gave him a long kiss. I never saw them kiss before. I remembered one time when we came back from a two-week vacation and Papa met us at the depot. He looked at Mama as though he could eat her up and Mama blushed. I thought he might kiss her, but instead, he touched her arm lightly and picked up the suitcases and we walked home.

Mama told us to go out in the waiting room while she stayed at his bedside. It wasn't long before she came out with a nun to tell us that Papa had passed away. We were in a daze. Nothing seemed real. I couldn't believe Papa would leave us.

The nun took us in a sunny room and gave us hot chocolate and cookies. When we had finished, Mama stood up, took a deep breath, squared her shoulders, and said, "Come on, kids, it's time to go home."

The coffin rested on a metal stand in our living room surrounded by flowers. The shades were drawn making the house gloomier than ever. Relatives and friends talked in hushed tones - doing whatever needed to be done in slow motion. Ida came in while I was wiping dishes and grabbed the towel. She wiped her eyes and blew her nose.

"He was such a wonderful man," she said as Ruth and Rod joined us. We all cried together using the dish towel to wipe away our tears and our runny noses. As I took the towel and turned back to finish the dishes, Ruth grabbed it from me. She threw it in the dirty clothes basket. We looked at one another and smiled.

I stared at the closed coffin as the minister started the service. Everything was blurry to my tear-filled eyes. He intoned Papa's fine character and many accomplishments. He read many familiar verses from the Bible. He assured us Papa would find his place in Heaven.

I cried harder than ever because I'm not so sure. The minister wasn't within ear-shot when Papa cussed. He didn't hear him say "God damn it!" at the slightest provocation.

"Thou shalt not use the name of thy Lord in vain," the words of my Sunday School teacher kept going through my head. I worry that Papa might not pass through Heaven's gates. I weep. The minister's words are no consolation.

Two weeks after the funeral, Aunt Mayme walked in with a bushel basket filled with home-canned vegetables, a bag of potatoes and a dressed chicken. She knew all of the insurance money was gone, spent for medical and burial expenses, and that we had nothing to live on. Mama sat at the table, her head bent.

The room was dark as Mama still insisted on keeping the shades down. We still talked in whispers and we weren't allowed to read the funny papers. (Although Ruth sometimes snuck them upstairs telling us, "Papa won't care if we read them".)

Aunt Mayme looked around the gloomy room. She walked to a window, pulled sharply on the shade, then let go. Flap, flap, BANG! She went to the other window, pulled roughly on the shade, then released it. The flapping noise and the loud BANG startled us. The room was filled with rays of sunshine.

"Speak up you kids. What's the matter with you? Are you afraid you're going to wake the dead?" Aunt Mayme shouted. Our genteel aunt sounded like a raucous stranger.

"Carrie, what are you going to do? Are you going to get a job?" She said in a loud, firm voice to Mama.

Mama moved her hands in a hopeless gesture, and shook her head. The truth was, Mama was a homebody. Papa and us kids did the errands and the shopping. Mama was shy and didn't go out very often.

"If you don't get a job, you'll have to take the children out of school and put them to work," Aunt Mayme went on in a matter-of-fact way.

This was a common practice and Rod, Ruth and I knew it was a possibility. Ida's father pulled her out of school and got her a job at a furniture factory. Ida didn't want to drop out of school but had to do what her father said. Lots of kids our age were working—and their parents collected every cent of the wages.

Mama's face turned a bright red at Aunt Mayme's suggestion. She was riled because Papa's family all graduated from high school and some went on to Normal School to become teachers, while Mama, with only a few years of formal schooling, placed a higher value on education.

"That's out of the question, Mayme, I want the kids to graduate," Mama said quite loudly. It surprised me because Mama was usually intimidated by Aunt Mayme who was inclined to be bossy and a "know-it-all". Sometimes I was told, "You're just like your Aunt Mayme," but it didn't bother me because I still admired her.

"Your slip is showing," Papa would say to me when we had

company and I was acting smarty. Even though he smiled, it was the clue that I was acting like Aunt Mayme and that I should be quiet.

"Some friends have asked about a job for me at Shurtleff's Candy Factory but I haven't felt up to going over there yet," Mama explained.

"Well you'd better apply, Carrie, and remember you're entitled to a Mother's Pension. You'll have to go to City Hall to apply," Aunt Mayme went on. Mama's head drooped.

When I saw how fearful Mama was, I thought of what Papa said to me on his death bed.

Without saying a word to anyone, I ran out the door to the City Hall only a few blocks away. I walked up the marble steps. They seemed awfully high to me. I wondered if that's how it was when you become a grown-up—if everything is steeper and more difficult. I entered the cold building.

"Where can I apply for a Mother's Pension?" I asked the first person I saw. The man's eyebrows shot up but he led me down the long hall and pointed to a room. I walked in, sat down and explained to the friendly, grey-haired woman why I was there. She asked me some questions, writing down the information.

"Tell your mother she will be receiving a check for twenty five dollars the first of every month." She smiled reassuringly.

I ran home and found Aunt Mayme was gone. Mama was still crumpled over the table.

"Mama, I went to City Hall and applied for the pension. The lady said you'll be getting a check for twenty five dollars the first of every month!" I shouted, tickled pink that I could do it for her.

She looked at me, full in the face, for a long time. I wondered if she was angry with me. Then I saw just a hint of a smile.

"You're growing up, Margie. Thank you." Mama said, patting my hand. I didn't feel grown up. I missed Papa—he was my anchor. I kept looking down the street expecting him to come back. Still I knew we had to go on without him. I had a new responsibility.

"I'll do what I can, Mama," I said.

Mama pushed her chair back from the table. She stood up facing away from me. She took a deep breath and squared her shoulders.

"Tomorrow, I'll go to Shurtleff's and apply for work," she announced in a loud, firm voice.

From Tomboy to GRAMMA